# CHRIST IN THE TWENTIETH CENTURY

# CHRIST
## IN THE
# TWENTIETH CENTURY

A SPIRIT CHRISTOLOGY

*by*

NORMAN HOOK
*Dean of Norwich*

LONDON
LUTTERWORTH PRESS

*First published 1968*

COPYRIGHT © 1968 NORMAN HOOK

*Lutterworth Press, 4 Bouverie Street, London, E.C.4*

7188 1370 7

*Printed in Great Britain by*
*Richard Clay (The Chaucer Press) Ltd., Bungay, Suffolk*

# Contents

| | Page |
|---|---|
| *Foreword* | 7 |
| Chapter | |
| 1. CHRIST'S REVELATION OF GOD | 11 |
| 2. EARLY ATTEMPTS IN CHRISTOLOGY | 34 |
| 3. THE LOGOS CHRISTOLOGY | 48 |
| 4. A SPIRIT CHRISTOLOGY | 61 |
| 5. THE RESURRECTION | 80 |
| 6. THE GOSPELS AND A SPIRIT CHRISTOLOGY | 104 |
| BOOKS CITED IN THE TEXT | 123 |
| INDEX | 125 |

## Foreword

WE ARE LIVING in an era which demands radical rethinking of some of the categories in which the faith of the Church has been expressed. This process of rethinking has begun, and will continue for many years to come. At the moment it would appear to produce results which strike many people as destructive of the Faith, and particularly in the field of New Testament Studies which, at the moment, are clouded with historical scepticism. There is likely to be a reaction against this state of affairs, and indeed the signs of it are becoming evident. So, present thesis will be followed by antithesis, and in turn this will give place to a synthesis which will commend itself as the truth to reasonable men.

Probably the most widespread criticism by ordinary people, as well as by the theologians, concerns the problem of the person of our Lord. The classical language of the creeds is no longer meaningful to people of our day, who suspect that the notion of God becoming man is an incredible one, belonging to the mythology of a bygone age. In a book of essays in honour of H. H. Farmer (*Prospect for Theology*) the writer of the Christological essay entitles it 'Christology at the crossroads'. This suggests that studies in this field do not know which road into the future to take. Actually, very little constructive thinking has been achieved about this difficult subject for many years, but I would judge that an outstanding contribution is W. R. Matthews' *The Problem of Christ in the Twentieth Century*—a book which sees the importance of modern psychology, and the meaning of Christ in terms of inspiration. Without working it out, Matthews believes that the answer lies in a Spirit Christology. This essay of mine attempts a further look at the possibility of such a Christology. It is properly an essay, rather than an exercise in precise theological scholarship, and, as such, I hope it may be helpful to clergymen and ministers, as well as readable by others. Just because it is an essay, I have refrained from cluttering up the text with detailed references, which otherwise should have been made. But this does not excuse me from acknowledging my indebtedness to many others, and this I would gratefully acknowledge.

The opening chapter is concerned with Christ's doctrine of God, remarkable alike in its balance, sublimity, and originality, and which demands an answer to the mystery of his person. It is right to be reminded of what Christ taught, in view of the fact that doctrines of God are now circulating which part company with it. For me, no one has so successfully interpreted Christ's doctrine of God as did William Temple in his various writings. A devotional summary of his mature thought is to be found in his *Personal Religion and the Life of Fellowship*, which was published as far back as 1936. To all his work, and to this little gem in particular, I am deeply indebted.

The second chapter reviews what his earliest followers thought of Jesus, ending with the Logos doctrine of the Fourth Gospel.

The third chapter provides a brief review of the fortunes

## FOREWORD

of this doctrine, and its final formulation at the Council of Chalcedon in A.D. 451.

Though I strongly dissent from his conclusions, I have found Paul van Buren's *The Secular Meaning of the Gospel* an unusally clear and competent guide, and I express gratitude for his concise and accurate thinking as set out in Part 1 of his book, pp. 25-85.

The chapter following, which deals with a Spirit Christology, owes something to the essayists who contributed to the volume, *The Spirit*, which was edited by B. H. Streeter in 1919. This is an old book which contains material of real value for the contemporary debate, and perhaps it is worth remarking that the thinking of previous generations should not be ignored. But most of all I am in deep debt to the work of W. R. Matthews.

The Resurrection is not only crucial to the existence of the Christian religion, but important also for a sound judgment on the question of the authenticity of the gospels. Obviously it has a bearing on the whole supernatural factor in the gospels. This chapter looks at the resurrection in the light of a Spirit Christology, and a conservative judgment here leads to a conservative judgment in regard to the credibility of the gospel material. Some attention is given to this problem in the concluding chapter.

I would try to forestall criticism, which might be tempted to dismiss the thesis of this essay on the ground that it is no more than a revival of the heresy of Paul of Samosata. I have taken pains to point out that the relation of the Spirit to Jesus was not a case of gradual possession, as with Paul of Samosata, but, as with St Luke, 'from the womb'. I have argued that both in respect of his revelation of God, and of

God's work in and through him, the values of a Spirit Christology are identical with the values of the Logos Christology. I would hold that the uniqueness of Jesus as one whose human spirit was united to the divine Spirit from the very beginning, is as impregnable as the uniqueness of the enfleshed Logos.

A Spirit Christology would demand some restatement of the doctrine of the Godhead—a notoriously difficult matter, and one about which a more discreet man might have kept silent. But I believe that a Spirit Christology, which would be rid of the ties of an outmoded Platonic philosophy, could well open the door to a doctrine of the Godhead which would commend itself to rational men of our own day and age.

NORMAN HOOK

CHAPTER ONE

## CHRIST'S REVELATION OF GOD

MAN has always believed in God, beginning with childish notions gradually outgrown, and followed by a period of readjustment occasioning perplexity. This in turn is followed by a noble idea of God such as befits the mature mind, or, at times, by the rejection of the God idea altogether. What we see happening in the history of the race is often the same evolution in the mind of the individual. Men begin life with childish notions of God which they outgrow, and then there follows a period of readjustment which leads to a worthy and mature conception of God, or, in a few cases, to the rejection of the idea altogether. So far as the modern scene is concerned, we may note that atheism still exists, but it has largely given place to the more modest doctrine of agnosticism, which holds that human knowledge by its very nature is limited, and that, therefore, the knowledge of ultimate reality is beyond our reach.

Most people, in the West at any rate, subscribe to what is historically called Theism, namely, to the belief that God is a personal spiritual being with whom it is possible to come into personal relations. There are many reasons which have accounted for a belief in Theism. At one time three famous arguments were employed to prove the existence of God— the cosmological argument, which held that God exists because the universe exists; the ontological argument, which held that because the idea of God exists, it must have a ground; and the teleological argument, which pointed to evidence everywhere in Nature of a benevolent design. These arguments still appeal to the ordinary man who does not profess to be a philosopher, but since the days of Kant such arguments have been under fire and have ceased to interest philosophers. They have contributed, no doubt, to men's belief in God, but there are other less tangible influences which have always been at work, influences which arise out of the experience of life itself, and not primarily from reasoning processes. Thus, certain values, particularly power, righteousness, love, justice, have always ranked high in human experience. These are the things which appeal to us as of supreme worth, and God is the embodiment or personalization of values which men live by, and have felt cannot be accounted for on purely natural lines. Indeed, they have felt that in some way they are continuous with MORE of the same quality. This divine MORE is exterior to us, and yet we are in some way connected with it, in some kind of harmony with it, and upon this harmony our peace and security rest. To this spiritual world men have given the name God, and as values are meaningless apart from personality, they have inferred that they witness to a personal God.

But it is often the poets who best interpret the experience of ordinary men, as when Wordsworth spoke of 'a presence that disturbs us with the joy of elevated thoughts, a sense sublime of something far more deeply interfused, whose dwelling is the light of setting suns, and the round ocean, and the living air, and the blue sky, and in the mind of man; a

## CHRIST'S REVELATION OF GOD

motion and a spirit that impels all thinking things, all objects of all thought, and rolls through all things'. In the deep realm of feeling, argument is often superfluous, and there are many who will say that God exists, just because they know that He exists.

But not all ideas of God admit the precision of Theism, and that applies not only to the oriental religions with their impersonal ideas of God but to some current thinking in our own day. One can read of 'the death of God'—an offensive expression which questions the validity of Theism. But there can be no question of the validity of Theism so far as Christianity is concerned, for Christianity is not a philosophy but a religion, resting its claims on what God is alleged to have done. Its fundamental premiss is that God can only be known if He has made himself known, which is no more than an obvious truism. It claims that God has made Himself known in the man Jesus. The claim may be true or false, but upon it the whole Christian edifice rests, and if it is true, there can be no question mark in connection with the word 'Theism'. The claim rests on the degree of authority belonging to the remarkable doctrine of God which Christ gave us, and it seems important to state it briefly as a norm by which contemporary thinking should be judged.

\* \* \*

We have to begin by reflecting that whatever be the full truth about Jesus, he was a child of his age who inherited the beliefs of his fathers. He belonged to a people whose doctrine of God, in respect of moral and spiritual sublimity, immeasurably surpassed the doctrines of God held by other peoples. This is a historical fact which demands explanation, and, if we look at the history of this people, the first thing which will strike us is that they make claims which seem peculiar. They regarded themselves as especially chosen by God to be the recipients of His self-revelation. They were the People of God, the chosen race, a 'peculiar' people—all of which sounds egocentric. They believed that between themselves and God there was a close and intimate relationship, which they described in the terms of a covenant. This covenant was no exclusive affair; it existed for the benefit of all peoples, and it was her failure in this solemn trusteeship which eventually led to Israel's rejection. The basis of this covenant notion was the incidence of certain outstanding people called the prophets, who claimed that God spoke through them, and claimed it with such conviction that they could declare 'Thus saith the Lord'. Their claim can only be tested by the quality of their revelation. What emerged through these men was a doctrine of God of such high and noble stature that it remains unparalleled by any other people. It is for that reason that their message has to be taken seriously. True, it is set in the thought-forms of an age far remote from ours, but its significance remains an outstanding fact in the history of the human race.

Christ, then, did not live and work amongst a people who were ignorant of God; His revelation came to a people who were capable, by their long training, of appreciating its meaning. They were already equipped with a knowledge of God, of which the following were the main elements:

(1) The Creator is the absolute being, complete, perfect, unrestricted, and wholly independent. Yet creation is an expression of His nature and being. 'Thou hast created all

things, and for thy pleasure they are, and were created' (Rev. 4:11). Ultimately there is no power but His power. In some sense, He is the doer of all that is done, and, in their insistence on the absolute sovereignty of God, the prophets at times use language which startles us. One of them can say 'I form the light and create darkness; I make peace and create evil' (Is. 45:7). Yet, to this teaching of the divine absoluteness there are certain qualifications. It is recognized that God has created men free agents, and that to this extent He has limited Himself. But the limitation is His own choice, and not by any external powers of compulsion, and the day will come which will exhibit the victory of His gracious purposes, so that there will be no doubt about His complete sovereignty at the end. It is also recognized that His omnipotence is not arbitrariness; it must correspond with certain principles of order and justice which have their seat in His own being. It would be illegitimate, therefore, to deduce a theology from an isolated saying such as 'God creates evil'. We must interpret this in its context as a bold and vivid expression on the part of the prophet, who is concerned to proclaim the absolute sovereignty of God.

(2) This God is a personal will. He is no mere abstract quality to contemplate, but 'the living God', who wills and disapproves, and judges, and hates, and loves, and blesses. If this is a case of conceiving God in human terms, yet, in so far as it deliberately chooses personality rather than some abstract principle to describe the reality of God, it is legitimate.

(3) This God is morally perfect. He is 'of purer eyes than to behold iniquity', inexorably and perfectly just. With Him there is no respect of persons, no such favouritism as

would lead Him to ignore anyone's sin, and no possibility of error in His judgments, for He sees into men's hearts and knows their inmost thoughts. Yet this God, who is so awful in His holiness, not only commands and judges but yearns over His people with a fatherly love. He is 'afflicted in their afflictions'. Moreover, this love of His is a jealous love capable of wrath.

(4) This God works in history in the fulfilment of His purposes. His hand is behind all that happens in judgment or in blessing. Nothing ultimately succeeds which flouts His will, and only when men obey Him can things go right in their own lives and in the world at large.

(5) He is 'the High and Lofty one that inhabiteth eternity'. We may note at this point the strong stress, everywhere expressed in the Old Testament, on the fact and importance of the divine transcendency. It is an affirmation that reality is not confined to this temporal sphere, which is marked by change and death, but that 'above' and 'beyond' this finite sphere there is the eternal realm of God, where the accidents of time do not belong. And we should appreciate the vital religious significance for man on this insistence on the divine transcendence, for obviously, without it, there can be no hope of immortality or eternal life for finite beings.

(6) It is noticeable how reticent the Hebrews were about ascribing to God any image. No proper name must be ascribed to Him; He is Jahweh, 'He who is', the living God. In the Old Testament God is rarely called 'Father', and this is due, no doubt, to aversion from images in any way connected with the sexual cults of Canaanite Nature worship.

(7) From this doctrine of God there emerges a particular doctrine of man. He is a creature made in the image of God,

and is described as a son of God. As such he is a being of dignity and worth, surpassing every other species of created life. He is empowered to subdue the earth and to exercise dominion over it; but he is warned that his role is to be a partner with God, for he is to remember that 'the earth is the Lord's and the fulness thereof'. He must not, therefore, transgress the bounds of his habitation. If he aspires to be as God, there will be Babel, which spells confusion and the nemesis of despair. Christ was very particularly concerned about this danger, and he feared for men the dread possibility of Hell. Hell is what happens when men choose to get along without God, when they claim the creation and ignore the Creator, when they seize the dominion and forget who conferred it. If we translate this into our modern situation, we can say there is nothing wrong about scientific exploration, for the Biblical charter bade man to replenish the material creation and to subdue it, and promised the divine blessing in so doing. But the peril of the modern situation is the peril which the Bible condemns, and about which Christ was so deeply concerned—the peril of forgetting the sovereignty of God.

(8) In spite of the fact of evil in creation, the Hebrews insisted that God is wholly good, 'of purer eyes than to behold iniquity'. This demanded some explanation of the mystery of evil. If it was contrary to the will of God, its origin must be assigned to the influence of a personal will in rebellion against God. This personal evil will they identified with the devil, or Satan. If this seems a fantastic notion, a case of unwarrantable personalization, at least it has the merit of offering an explanation in a sphere where other explanations are conspicuous by their absence, or which are no

explanation at all. At least it does justice to the feeling shared by many that the potency of evil lies outside the sphere of human sources.

Such, in brief outline, was the thought of God possessed by the people to whom our Lord came. They claimed that it was a knowledge of God which was something far more than mere human speculation. They believed that it had been revealed and declared by the prophets, and its most marked characteristic is never that it afforded material for speculation about the Godhead, but that it demanded response in appropriate action.

★  ★  ★

What, then, did Christ add to this doctrine of God? He recalled people to the teaching of the prophets and repudiated the thought of God which had come to prevail in his day. That thought was summarized by Harnack in these words:

> *They* thought of God as a despot guarding the ceremonial observancies in His household; *he* breathed in the presence of God. *They* saw Him only in the law, which they had converted into a labyrinth of dark defiles, blind alleys and secret passages; *he* saw and felt Him everywhere. *They* were in possession of a thousand of His commandments, and thought therefore that they knew Him; *he* had only one, and knew Him by it. *They* had made this religion into an earthly trade, and there was nothing more detestable; *he* proclaimed the living God and the soul's nobility (*What is Christianity?* pp. 50-51).

In this quotation Harnack contrasts the Judaism of our Lord's day with the religion of the prophets to which Jesus recalled men. On the whole, the monotheistic tendency of the Old Testament is to stress a sublime transcendency, with less feeling for the immanency of the divine within creation. The sublimities of nature are not seen as instinct with the presence of God, but rather serve to enhance the measureless power of God. They are as nothing compared with Him. 'Behold He taketh up the isles as a very little thing.' 'The hills melt like wax at the presence of God.' One gets the picture of an omnipotence enthroned in the heavens which is remote from the ways and thoughts of men. God created the world and all that therein is, but He stands apart from it.

But it would be untrue to say that there is no thought in the Old Testament of the divine immanence. It was the influence of the prophets which restored the balance, and this influence is seen particularly in the psalms which very frequently speak of the tender relationship which can exist between man and God. He who dwells in the high and lofty place can 'draw nigh unto them that are of a broken heart'. Moreover, the prophets saw a vital link between God and man in the thought of the Spirit of God. They thought of creation as the work of the Spirit. Extraordinary endowments of body or leadership are due to the 'invasion' of the Spirit. Wisdom and discernment are especially gifts of the Spirit, and so is prophecy. The Spirit of the Lord can 'come upon' or 'rest upon' a man so that he is able to declare the Word of the Lord. This teaching of the prophets went far to see God as immanent in the world, and most of all in the human sphere, as well as being transcendent of the world.

The thought of the Spirit of God is of course a way of thinking of God in action. There is no notion here of any mediator to bridge the gulf between God and man. But in the period between the Testaments the influence of the prophets had waned, and in particular this thought of the Spirit of God. The need was felt for some mediator between God and man, and in this period angelology had found a place in Judaism through Persian influence. Greek influence was also at work, for Philo, the Alexandrian Jew, had taken over the Greek concept of the Logos, the indwelling reason of the universe, and had personalized it. The Logos as the indwelling deity was knowable, whilst God himself remained unknowable. The same tendency is seen in the idea of the Wisdom of God, also personalized. But the immediacy of personal relations between God and man seems to have been wellnigh lost in the period represented by the Judaism of our Lord's day, and the recovery of this and its enrichment in warmth and vital meaning was one of the achievements of Jesus. In this sense Harnack was right when he saw Jesus returning to the teaching of the prophets.

But in many ways Jesus challenged the teaching of the past. He certainly did not think of creation as something completed from which God now stands apart. According to the writer of the Fourth Gospel he says, 'My Father worketh hitherto, and I work.' He saw God ceaselessly active in sustaining His creation. The Old Testament, as we have seen, is exceedingly chary of ascribing any image to God, and this was taken very seriously by the Judaism of our Lord's day. But Jesus had a very definite image of God in the thought of the Abba Father. But the great difference which Jesus made was a complete difference in ethos. God is no longer remote but always accessible. There is no need of any thought of a mediator, for God is the Father who loved us before we loved Him, and who is always immediately approachable. He is to be recognized not only in the great events of history, and not only in the exploits of the few. Everything in existence speaks of Him, not only nature in all her moods but the secular affairs of men in so far as they are legitimate.

Frequently it was to the ordinary everyday affairs of men that Jesus turned when he wanted to teach something about God. This was a new approach and in stark contrast to that of the Judaism of his day. God for him was the loving Father, and this intensified to a new degree the thought of God's personal love of individuals, good and bad alike, Jew and Gentile alike. His thought retains the familiar notions represented by such epithets as king, lawgiver, and judge, but each of them became aspects of God's fatherhood. Into this thought of fatherhood he poured such warmth and wealth of meaning, that, when the Evangelists try to reproduce it, they combine the Aramaic with the Greek. He is the Abba Father. No prophet had gone so far as to say that God is as good to the wicked as to the righteous. This shocked the Judaism of his day, but behind it there is the insistence that God's love infinitely transcends our poor human notions of what love is. We are to 'be perfect as He is perfect', to bless those who curse us, and to love those who hate us, for only so may we be worthy children of our heavenly Father.

In the moral sphere he elevated the Deuteronomic precept of loving God with all members, and neighbour as self, into the first of all commandments. What was new about such teaching was the new emphasis he put upon the old, and the way in which this was so signally displayed in his own living. He added himself, for nothing is more remarkable than the perfection of love which is there to be seen. He loved for better and for worse, for richer and for poorer, in sickness and in health, throughout every moment of his life, and supremely in his death. Such love has been seen in this world neither before nor since. Yet it was never merely sentimental, for always it reflected in complete equipoise those two facets of the prophetic teaching, which seem to us difficult to reconcile—the thought of the awful sovereignty of God and His stern judgment, and the thought of the tender love of God, who is afflicted in the afflictions of His people.

In Jesus these seemingly contradictory elements are reconciled into a harmonious whole. Thus, we find a stern note in this love of his, which properly belongs to the idea of a perfect love. Against all that denied God's gracious purposes and put stumbling-blocks in the way of His children, Jesus uttered the sternest denunciations. Against all parade of pride and selfishness, he used the strongest language, and, morally, this is a mark of perfect love, not a weakness to be criticized. And, perhaps the most significant of all features of this divine love is its amazing humility—a thought which should check any temptation to easy-going familiarity. It is a love which stoops to perform the menial act of service. One of the New Testament writers, reflecting on all this, wrote that 'God is love'. When Christ was asked which is the first and great commandment, he quoted that great word of the Old Testament: 'Thou shalt love God with all thy soul, heart, and mind, and thy neighbour as thyself.'

Here is the implicit recognition that living and loving are one and the same thing. Love is a kind of measure or foot-rule of our humanity, i.e. of our reality as persons. But, this truth that 'God is love' did not come to the Christian religion by any process of philosophical speculation; it came by revelation, and most of all by the fact that Jesus 'added himself'.

But the truth that God is love suggests also the purpose of our existence, which is that we may 'love Him and enjoy Him for ever'. The response which we ought to make to Him is the response which Christ made—a love and trust gladly rendered, and an obedience which never faltered. But, the fact that we are impotent to do so is the mystery of our human sinfulness. Its tragic seriousness is that it alienates us from God, which is eternal death. It was into this state of affairs which is our human predicament, that the God who is love sent His Christ. He lived as a man amongst men, and in all respects he was a real human being, save that he had none of the limitations of a nature tainted by any form of sinfulness. His mission was to remove that barrier between man and God, which is caused by that sinfulness which comes, in part at least, from man's impotency.

The New Testament uses various words to do justice to the work which Christ alone could accomplish—such words as atonement, satisfaction, expiation, propitiation. Each of them has something to contribute to the truth, but none by itself is adequate, and there is one word, the word 'propitiation', which in its modern sense should never be used. A broken love can be expiated, and indeed must be expiated before there can be reconciliation, but it cannot be propitiated.

The heart of Christ's work lay in the expiation he made for us, which we could never make for ourselves. To this end he identified himself with our human estate to the utmost limit, even to the extremity of physical death. His expiation was the sacrifice of a perfect obedience, which he could offer, but which we, in our sinful estate, could never offer. He made on our behalf that acknowledgment of God's holiness, and of the righteousness of His judgment on our sin, which we ought to make but cannot make. What he did in love for us provides the ethos of Christian living. Such love is to be reflected in our lives, and the sin of sins is therefore lovelessness. William Temple wrote:

> Do you believe—vitally and emotionally believe—that the Creator is the Redeemer, that Jesus Christ reveals the ultimate reality? I don't. My mind believes; my conscience approves; but my heart is also set on too much else to trust effectively. And if it were not that the Creator-Redeemer both can and does offer Himself to dwell within us and make us like himself, I should neither have faith in God, nor hope for the world. Though all my lower nature shrinks from the sacrifice it must face, yet in our best moments we know that the one satisfaction of our souls is to be found in their surrender to Jesus Christ, that he may shape them into the likeness of his perfect love, and that the accomplishment of this for mankind is the one means of purging out of the world all that now spoils and embitters life (*Personal Religion and the Life of Fellowship*, pp. 13 and 14).

All this, and much more, might be said in illustration of the fact that Jesus 'added himself' to the beliefs of his fathers.

\*　　\*　　\*

But the heart of his teaching about God was centred in the thought of the Kingdom. There are many aspects and insights which belong to the richness of his thought about the

## CHRIST'S REVELATION OF GOD

Kingdom of God, but there is one in particular which is particularly apposite for our own day. The Kingdom of God relates to the rule of God. That 'the earth is the Lord's and the fulness thereof' is one of the great affirmations which Christ took over from his own people. All the legitimate activities of men derive ultimately from the earth and from what God provides. It follows, therefore, that all legitimate secular interests of man represent the will of God. But because 'the earth is the Lord's' man's dependence on God must be acknowledged and honoured. He is the Lord of all life, and it is His Kingship which must prevail if man is to enjoy that status and fullness of life which God wills for him. When all man's secular activities are thus subject to, and directed by the rule of God, then the Kingdom is present and the life of that Kingdom is eternal life.

It is important to appreciate that Christ's teaching about the Kingdom was no retreat from life, no mere species of other-worldliness. It was not a case of separating the secular from the sacred, but of realizing the sacred in and through the secular. And so we find that he was concerned to state the principles which determine the will of God in and through the secular sphere.

To attempt to state, or even to summarize, these principles cannot be undertaken here, for it would demand a large volume in itself. All we can do is to note a few instances of the distinctive insights which Christ provided.

He taught, for example, that it is incompatible with the reign of God that there should be any insistence on privilege, any claiming of rank, or the right to be served and obeyed. The only title to rank and authority which the Kingdom recognizes is meekness and humble service—a title which becomes non-existent on the very first attempt of its possessor to exact its recognition.

All men are to be treated as brothers, and this involves the duty of foregiveness 'until seventy times seven'. This is no mere role of passivity, for abhorrence of sin and pity for the sinner must so work in him, who seeks the rule of God, as to impel him to every means that may help the offender to a state of redemption.

The principle of retaliation is prohibited; violence is not to be met with violence, nor litigation answered by litigation. Here again, what is enjoined is not passivity but something active. No way is so effective in meeting evil conduct as when the victim receives his ill-treatment without resentment, and continues to welcome every opportunity to serve his aggressor.

All this is revolutionary, and far removed from the usual ways of men, but it is the most practical of all methods for those whose first aim is the establishment of the reign of God. Evil is not to be fought with its own weapons; the only weapon which God approves is the force of love and trust in His good purposes. Those who follow this way will find that all necessary things are added unto them.

\* \* \*

All we have attempted here is a mere glimpse at teaching of the most far-reaching social implications, all of which has something to teach us about God.

In his *Guide to the Debate about God* (1965), David Jenkins sees as one of the fundamental issues in the contemporary debate the question as to how far the universe provides data for a belief in God. There can be no doubt that the teaching of Jesus assumes that it certainly does, and Christian thinkers have always witnessed to this truth. But a new idea was propounded in the eighteenth century by Schleiermacher, who held that religion must resign all claims on science. He made this concession to science in an effort to attract the enlightened men of his day to a serious consideration of the claims of religion. He has been followed in this surrender by such moderns as Bultmann, Barth, and Brunner, all of whom have validated their religious belief on subjective or existentialist grounds. In the case of Bultmann and many who have been influenced by him, the effect has been to produce a historical scepticism in regard to the gospels, which goes far to imperil the claims of the Christian religion to be a historical religion. The notion of God intervening in history, of the supernatural seen in association with the natural, does not accord with the thesis that the world provides no data for belief in God. In that case the supernatural must be denied and the gospels de-mythologized.

On the other hand, Bonhoeffer was not prepared to surrender the world to the scientists, believing that God was to be found in and through the secular. This has led to another feature of the contemporary debate, where the religious is virtually identified with the secular. It sees no need to go outside or beyond this world for its belief in God, for, if God is not to be found in the secular and in the depths of man's being, He is to be found nowhere. This point of view avoids the subjectivism of the existentialists but shares their suspicion of the supernatural.

It would appear then that this is fundamentally a debate about transcendence and immanence, and that behind it is the problem of how we are to think of the creation. If you surrender the claims of religion to science, you accept the premiss of science that the universe is a closed system, which contains within itself the explanation of everything that happens or can happen within it. This in turn decides the content of knowledge. Whatever is amenable to scientific proof is knowledge, and what lies outside it is mere opinion. If you continue to believe in God, you can do no more than validate your belief on purely subjective lines, and the whole category of the supernatural must go, including apparently the idea for which the word 'Theism' stands. A recent phase of this type of thought can even use such language as 'the death of God'.[1]

But this kind of thinking bears no relation to the thought of Christ. For him, the world is God's world, and the higher achievements of man, so far from being independent of God, derive ultimately from Him.

It appears, then, that Schleiermacher started a hare which has seriously run off course, and it may help us to see straight about this problem of transcendence and immanence, if we glance at the thought of two distinguished men of the recent past.

C. S. Lewis, in his *Surprised by Joy* (1955), gives us an account of his spiritual pilgrimage. The interest of it is that it is the story of a pilgrimage from atheism to Christianity. At one time Lewis would not have wished to quarrel with the point of view of Schleiermacher, which, he would have contended, fitted in very well with his atheism. But he describes in this book (Chap. 13) how he came to the conclusion that mind was no late-comer to the universe, no

[1] See Note at end of this chapter.

mere epiphenomenon, but that the whole universe was, in the last resort, an expression of the mind of God. This led him to the concept of the Absolute Mind, and to the thought that what we see and experience here is 'appearance'— 'appearance' of the Absolute. The next step was the identification of the Absolute with the personal God. The universe for him did indeed provide data for belief in God, and so he arrived at a point of view which embraced the teaching of Christ and brought him hope and joy. Lewis was concerned with the truth, and would have regarded surrender of the claims of religion to science as a betrayal of the truth.

So also would the distinguished philosopher, A. Seth Pringle Pattison, who reached a similar outlook. Reference may be made to his essay on *Transcendence and Immanence* in the volume, *The Spirit*, published in 1922, and edited by B. H. Streeter. He was concerned to be rid of a transcendency 'which seeks to magnify God's greatness by separating Him from the world, placing Him at a distance from it and making Him self-sufficient and complete without it' (p. 13). He is critical of what is called 'the cabinetmaker theory of creation'. God is its ever-present sustaining ground, and the universe only exists because He perpetually creates it. It belongs to the very nature of God to create. He is 'no *deus absconditus*, hidden, withdrawn from our sight, but a Creator that eternally utters Himself in and to His creatures' (p. 14). God's action is simply the realization of His nature, and this is the ideal of action, the perfect freedom which belongs to God alone. This means that God never existed without a creation in which He was manifested. Thus the essentially creative nature of God implies His immanence.

But also, the eternal contrast between the actual and the ideal furnishes the natural key to the problem of immanence and transcendence.

> Transcendence does not mean remoteness or aloofness. The distinction it points to is that between the perfect and the imperfect ... and by perfection we mean the perfect realization of those very values which we recognize as the glory and the crown of our human nature.... This idea of perfection disclosing its features gradually as men become able to apprehend the vision, is the immanent God, the inspiring Spirit, to whom all progress is due (p. 21-22).

But the immanent God is always the infinitely transcendent, the two aspects involving one another.

The merit of this thinking is that it provides a clear answer to the question of whether the world provides data for belief in God. It sees this answer in a firm grasp of the divine immanence and an equally firm grasp of the divine transcendence. Both men could see God in the secular, but they see the secular in terms of the supernatural which makes it meaningful. Both see God as allowing man to think His thoughts after Him, to unlock the secrets of His creation, and to stand amazed at its incredible grandeur and its miraculous contrivance.

The spate of books about secularization and secularism continues to flow, and there is need of a clear philosophy of the secular in its relation to the sacred. A helpful contribution has been made to this end by Charles Davis in his Maurice lectures, entitled *God's Grace in History*. After recognizing that a proper distinction should be made between secularization (the fact that secular processes exist) and secularism (the interpretation of these processes to the exclusion of the sacred or the transcendent), Davis argues for a frank recognition of the autonomy of the secular in its own sphere. He insists that to do this is to enhance rather than to harm the sacred, for it is no service to religion to bring in the transcendent to fill gaps which belong to the secular. 'Christianity unites the sacred and the secular in a unity of order, but it refuses to identify them' (p. 17).

Commenting on Bonhoeffer's controversial phrase 'religionless Christianity' as popularly understood, he believes it expresses two important insights, but in a falsely exclusive way: (1) It expresses an impatience with the notion of the institutional church turned in upon itself and concerned only with its own preservation. This is a proper protest, provided that it is remembered that it is an indispensable function of the church to manifest the presence of the sacred. (2) It emphasizes what Davis calls 'the indirect mission of the church', by which he means the duty of the church to get out of its insulated environment, and meet God's grace as it operates in the secular world. But it must not be forgotten that nature is not grace, and that 'the mission of the church can never be reduced to a supporting of the secular' (p. 89).

All this is no more than a reassertion of the implications of Christ's doctrine of God. It is indeed the most noble and heart-desiring of all doctrines of God. But is it true? Does it correspond to the reality of things? The answer to such questions depends on what is believed about the authority of Jesus who gave us this doctrine of God. Who was this man, and how are we to understand him?

## Note on 'Death of God'

The approach of such men as Lewis and Pringle Pattison, which is obviously in direct line with the outlook of Jesus, is in sharp contrast with the point of view associated with the contemporary 'Death of God' school of theologians. On the part of some, this phrase appears to mean no more than a rejection of theism, and so of supernaturalism. For van Buren theism is meaningless, but so also is atheism. Others seem to mean by the phrase, that so far as the secular culture of the world is concerned, God is as good as dead, which is an obvious truism, and an indictment of the spiritual blindness of secular culture. But, also, there are those who write as though God really did not exist, but who see Jesus as 'the man for others'; but in their case they cannot say he is 'the man for God'.

What is at stake is the issue of transcendence. The divine transcendency emphasizes the truth that God must not be identified with the finite and the temporal, else He ceases to be God. Transcendency does not mean making God an object. God is not a being amongst other beings; He is a Spirit of pure Being and the ground of all being, which means that a Christian is bound to be a supernaturalist. A Christian does not deny that the God who is 'beyond' the finite does not meet us in the depths of our being and in the challenge of our neighbour. Because he believes that the universe is instinct with the presence of God, he can find God everywhere, and most of all in the depths of his being.

We may agree that the discipline of philosophy, in so far as it helps to keep us on the road of truth, is important. But the definitions of particular philosophies do not necessarily comprise the full truth, and indeed sometimes distort it. The whole truth transcends any philosophy, and, in the end, it can only be stated in terms of paradox. God must not be conceived as one object amongst many. Philosophy has the right to say this in the cause of truth. At the same time, God is to be worshipped as one with whom we can commune on the personal level. That also belongs to the truth, and it yields a paradox which is inescapable.

CHAPTER TWO

## EARLY ATTEMPTS IN CHRISTOLOGY

A REMARKABLE doctrine of God proclaimed with authority, a man whose remarkable words were matched by remarkable deeds—who was this man? How was his genius to be explained, and how did he fit in with the rest of men? These were some of the questions which his followers had to ask themselves, and to which they found it necessary to give some sort of answer. They gave a variety of answers, all of them reflecting thoughts and hopes which are given expression in the Old Testament Scriptures. They said that he was the Messiah or Christ, that he was the Son of God, and they were bold enough even to ascribe to him the title 'Lord'. Towards the end of the century their thought had become more precise, for then they equated him with the Greek notion of the Logos, who had been made flesh in this Jesus.

Of one thing they never doubted—that he was a genuine human being like unto themselves, but they were also conscious that they must say more. One way in which they tried to see his significance was by describing him as the Messiah. The word means 'anointed', and in early days anointing was associated with kings and priests, and was a sign that God had chosen them for office, and a pledge that His Spirit would be with them.

In the Old Testament, the title 'Messiah' is never used with a future reference to the king whom God would one day raise up to rule over the restored kingdom of David. This notion first appears in Jewish writings in the period between the Testaments. In the 17th of the Psalms of Solomon (about 50 B.C.) reference is made to a king whom God will raise up to deliver His people and reign over them in righteousness. He will be strong 'in holy spirit', and overcome his enemies, not by military force but 'by the word of his mouth'. He would be free from sin and endued by God with wisdom and understanding.

It is legitimate to wonder how far this late notion of the Messiah influenced Jesus and his interpreters. In the Synoptic gospels Jesus never openly claims to be Messiah, and some argue that he himself never made such a claim. This, however, is to be doubted, for it is clear that at his trial before the Sanhedrin Jesus frankly admitted that he was the Christ (Mark 14:61f.), though, according to Matthew and Luke, he refused to give a direct answer. But his silence was taken as an admission that he was the Christ, and it was on the ground that he was a pretended Messiah, the King of the Jews, that he was put to death. In the Fourth Gospel, however, Jesus is acknowledged to be the Christ from the beginning of his ministry. This is in sharp conflict with the evidence of the Synoptic gospels, and on historical grounds there can be little doubt which source is to be preferred.

All we can say is that in Christian usage the title acquired a new and different meaning—a meaning which has affinities with the conception we have noted from the Psalms of Solomon, but enlarged and widened to cover the appeal which Jesus made, an appeal which transcended the merely materialistic confines of the Jews. Soon the title lost all meaning, for it had no interest to Gentiles. It simply became a proper name like 'Jesus' itself.

We may sum up the meaning of this title as applied to Jesus by observing that it tells us nothing of his relation to God. It emphasizes the fact that he was a genuine man, called of God to do His will, and to be endowed with the gift of His Spirit. No doubt in the Fourth Gospel the title has overtones which may make it mean more than this, but what we have said undoubtedly represents the outlook of the people to whom our Lord came. The majority of the people thought of Messiah as one of the line of David whom God would raise up to be king of a restored Davidic kingdom, and who would exercise physical force to achieve his ends. But alongside this notion there was the other notion of the Psalms of Solomon, which was also held by some. But how deeply it was influential we do not know, nor do we know whether Christ or his interpreters were influenced by it. In any case, the title 'Messiah', as was soon recognized, tells us little or nothing as to who Jesus was.

\* \* \*

Another title which is ascribed to Jesus is 'Son of God'. The title 'Messiah' would mean nothing to Gentiles, but the title 'Son of God' would, for they were accustomed to interpret all excellence and heroic achievements as manifestations of the divine. It is in this sense that Jesus was a manifestation of the divine, that the title is frequently used in the writings of St Paul and St John.

But the title has also an Old Testament background. The king or the high priest, as representing the people of the covenant, is occasionally called God's Son, as in 2 Sam. 7:14, where it is said of David, 'I will be his father, and he shall be my son.' But the relation here is not an ontological relation, but rather a relation of obedience. Israel itself is spoken of as God's son (e.g. Exod. 4:22), and what justifies this ascription is again the thought of serving obedience. The prophets lament Israel's disobedience and failure to fulfil its vocation of sonship. If Jesus used the title of himself, this would seem to be the sense in which he used it, namely, as one who was the obedient servant. As such he appears to have thought of himself as uniquely God's Son in whom God was well pleased. The emphasis is thus on what Jesus does, rather than on who he is.

The matter is taken further in the Pauline and Johannine writings, where increasing emphasis is laid on the unity of the Father and the Son. All things are now subject to the Son, that God may be all in all (1 Cor. 15:28). What is suggested here, though not defined, is something more than a relation of call and response, but a relation of ontological significance. Perhaps this was a natural transition, which would certainly be meaningful to Gentiles. If Jesus used this title of himself, it was probably in the Hebrew sense of the obedient servant. But whether he used it in the other sense is doubtful. But it was so used by his interpreters.

\* \* \*

Another title which is used of Jesus is 'Lord'. This is a title of divine significance, which would be intelligible to Gentiles who acknowledged 'gods many and lords many' (1 Cor. 8:5). In the Old Testament, apart from its use as a courtesy title it has a specialized use. It substituted the ineffable name of JHVH (Jahweh), which might not be uttered, but for which 'adonai' was spoken instead. 'Adonai' means 'Lord', and was translated as such by the Septuagint translators of the Hebrew Old Testament into Greek by their word 'kurios'. This is undoubtedly the sense in which we are to understand the ancient Aramaic prayer 'Maran atha'— 'O Lord come'—which witnesses to the earliest Christian confession 'Jesus is Lord'. So, the fact that the title would be readily intelligible to Greeks does not mean that it arose originally in Greek circles. It had an accepted meaning in Hebrew circles at the time of our Lord, which equated it with the divine.

Luke alone amongst the Synoptists records the title as being in general use during the ministry of Jesus, though Mark also records Jesus as quoting Psalm 11:1 in relation to himself. It was undoubtedly the resurrection which inspired the title, but this does not mean that belief in the Lordship of Jesus was not already grounded in historical experience. He had exercised lordship in his dealings with men and in his handling of disease, and this may well have inspired the title during his lifetime.

It is not difficult to understand how Gentile Christians came to give Jesus this divine title, but much more difficult to understand how Jewish Christians could reconcile such a title with their strict monotheism. But this they did in the sense that everything a man may expect from God he may expect equally from Jesus. Their thought is nowhere worked out, though it may be noticed in passing that St Paul appeared to maintain the subordination of the Son to the Father.

This word 'Lord' takes us much further theologically

than does the title 'Messiah' or the title 'Son of God'. In the Synoptic gospels there is no suggestion that Jesus is not regarded as a genuine human being, but there is a sense of something more to be included in the truth about him, which becomes more precisely defined after the resurrection, but not defined to a point which would satisfactorily answer the question as to who he was. The title 'Lord' really witnessed to the needs of religious experience rather than to any precise theological statement.

\* \* \*

The title 'Son of Man', which must have sounded as strange in Greek as it does in English, always occurs as a self-designation of Jesus. In the gospels it is never used by anyone except Jesus himself, and neither Jesus nor the Evangelists explain its meaning, or the reason for its use, nor do the people invite any explanation. All this poses a problem for which no completely satisfactory explanation has been found. Nor do we get much help from the use of the phrase in the Old Testament, where 'son of man' means simply 'a man'. The phrase occurs frequently in Ezekiel, as in 'Son of man, stand upon thy feet, and I will speak unto thee' (2:1), where, as elsewhere, it emphasizes the contrast between the human and the divine, and the dignity which God bestows upon man in choosing to speak with him.

The Aramaic equivalent of the Hebrew occurs in the book of Daniel in the well-known passage:

> I saw in the night visions, and, behold, there came with the clouds of heaven one like unto a son of man, and he came even to the ancient of days.... And there was given him dominion, and glory, and a kingdom (7:13f.).

The figure 'like a son of man' symbolizes the kingdom of the saints. It is not suggested that this man-like figure had any real existence outside the vision, any more than had the beast-like figures. In any case what is emphasized here is the humanity of the man-like figure. This passage can hardly account for the notion of the Messiah as a celestial figure who bore some special relation to God. This notion belongs to the apocalyptic book of Enoch, which exists only in an Ethiopic version, the history of which is very obscure. It is more than doubtful that Jesus should have chosen the title from this source, and it is much more likely that he took it from the Daniel passage, where the figure of 'one like unto a son of man' represents the holy community, which was the destined role of Israel. Israel had failed to fulfil her role, and Jesus saw himself as representing the holy community. He alone was now Son of Man.

Was Jesus, then, doing no more than indicating that he was a man? And are we to say that the claim that 'the Son of Man hath power on earth to forgive sins' means 'man hath power on earth to forgive sins'? This cannot be so, and it follows that 'Son of Man' must have had some original and specific meaning for Christ himself. It does not seem to have been a Messianic title in use at the time—not at least in the sense of Enoch as a superhuman figure in close relation with God. It is more probable that Jesus was influenced by the Daniel passage where 'son of man' is the embodiment of the holy community. 'Son of man' in this context could indicate, as it does sometimes in the Old Testament, the sense of '*the* Man'. Jesus, we may guess, thought of himself as *the* Man, the man who was the true representative of Israel, the suffering servant of Isaiah 53.

The title would thus include what the title 'Messiah' stood for, but it would be enriched by the thought of the one who represented others and suffered vicariously in their behalf. The title would possess all the advantages and none of the disadvantages of the title 'Messiah', which Jesus never openly used of himself. In a word, its meaning would witness to his mission.

As such it was undoubtedly a creation of Jesus, which, whilst witnessing to his manhood, tells us something more about him. But how much more it tells us is not made clear, though evidently in his own mind it included the right to forgive sins. It would be easier to account for this claim if Jesus had identified himself with the supernatural being of Enoch, who was not of human descent, but one who sat on the throne of God. But all the evidence seems to point to the fact that the Similitudes of Enoch exercised no influence on the people of our Lord's day, including Jesus himself.

\* \* \*

If we review the evidence thus far, what conclusions may be reached about it? Clearly Jesus is thought of as a genuine man, and the emphasis of such titles as Messiah, Son of God, and Son of Man tells us more of the role of Jesus rather than unlocks the mystery of who he is. But the Lord's own self-designation—Son of Man—is original, and allows us merely to glimpse into his own self-consciousness. We have to take account of his mysterious claim to forgive sins, which is a divine prerogative; we also have to take account of the fact that he exercised lordship over men, over disease, and over natural forces, and this, combined with the Easter event, throws some light on the title 'Lord', which, in the Pauline writings, identifies him with the Son who bears an ontological relation to the Father.

\* \* \*

Another type of language is used of him in the Johannine, Pauline, and Petrine writings, all of which may be said to be comment on the Logos doctrine. It is said that he who had seen Jesus 'had seen the Father' (John 14:9). He is said to be 'in the Father', and 'the Father in him'. It is said that 'God was in Christ, reconciling the world unto Himself' (2 Cor. 5:19). This suggests something about the mystery of his person which gave him the right to exercise a divine role. The same writer, St Paul, speaks of him as existing before he was born, and even before all creation, in a state of equality with God (Phil. 2:6). By becoming man 'he emptied himself'.

St Paul seems to admit a real subordination of the Son to the Father (1 Cor. 15:28), but he also constantly unites his name with that of the Father, as in the Grace of 2 Corinthians 13:14. The kind of language used by St Paul is by no means peculiar to him. Very similar language occurs in the Epistles of St Peter. The Epistle of St James calls him 'the Lord of glory' (2:1), whilst the Epistle to the Hebrews regards him as superior to the angels and the object of their worship (1:4-6).

It is interesting to note that nowhere, except perhaps in the Fourth Gospel, do the New Testament writers baldly speak of Jesus Christ as God. Yet they worship him without any precision of thought as to who he was. The Logos doctrine of St John, which appeared about the turn of the century, is, in a way, a logical expression of what faith in

## EARLY ATTEMPTS IN CHRISTOLOGY

him whom they called 'Lord' had come to mean. Here it is stated that the Word or Logos of God was made flesh in the person of Jesus called the Christ.

In the Old Testament the Word of God, or the Word of the Lord, simply means any communication made by God to men, especially through a prophet. When we read such expressions as The Lord 'sent his word, and healed them' (Ps. 107:20), this is no more than a literary personification. Evidence for a real personification of 'the Word of God' belongs to later Jewish thought, and is to be found in the Targums, the vernacular paraphrases of the Old Testament used in the synagogue worship.

In the New Testament, the phrase 'Word of the Lord' has all the meanings we find in the Old Testament, though its application is much wider, and often denotes the Christian message, as in Acts 13:44, where we read that 'almost the whole city was gathered together to hear the Word of God'. It is alone in the prologue of St John's Gospel that the word 'Logos' is an eternal divine person, through whom in the beginning, everything was made, and who is seen incarnate in Jesus Christ.

The evangelist assumes his readers to be familiar with this conception of the personal divine Logos, which is of Greek origin. In Greek thought, the Logos denotes the rational principle of the universe by which it is sustained. But Jewish thinkers, influenced no doubt by Greek philosophy, had reached a very similar conception in the notion of the Divine Wisdom. In Proverbs 8–9, for example, the personification of Wisdom is more than a mere literary device. Much later Jewish thinkers, writing in Greek, combined the two concepts, using by preference the concept of the Logos.

It was, therefore, easy for the Fourth Evangelist to take the further step of explaining Jesus by identifying him with the Logos of contemporary Greek and Hebrew thought.

The motive behind this further step was the missionary interest of the Church, but whether this Logos doctrine is the kind of doctrine we might have expected of Hebraic thought is doubtful, and whether it is the best way of answering the question as to who Jesus was, is also doubtful. Actually, the man who records Jesus as addressed by the title 'Lord', Gentile though he was, was a man thoroughly steeped in Hebrew tradition, and it is not surprising to find that in his writings, and to a lesser extent in the first and second gospels, there is an incipient Christology, which, if it had been developed, might have proved more satisfactory than the Logos doctrine which the Church chose as the basis of its thinking.

The incipient Christology of the Synoptists, and especially of St Luke, is a Spirit Christology, seeing the meaning of Christ's existence in terms of the activity of the Spirit of God. It was natural for the Jews to account for striking spiritual phenomena in terms of the Spirit of God, and this is evident in all the Synoptic gospels. Both Matthew and Luke see the birth of Jesus as by the instrumentality of the Spirit of God. Luke sees John Baptist as one who 'shall be filled with the Holy Ghost, even from his mother's womb' (1:15). Zacharius is also one who is filled with the Holy Ghost, and of Simeon it is said that 'the Holy Ghost was upon him'. All three gospels describe the baptism and temptation of Jesus as events motivated by the Holy Spirit. Luke describes Jesus as 'exulting in the Holy Spirit' (10:21), and this is a typically Lucan addition. In 4:16ff. we have

Luke's account of Jesus preaching in the Nazareth synagogue, where Jesus is reported as quoting Isaiah 61, and seeing himself as the fulfilment of this prophecy as one anointed by the Spirit of God. By the power of the Spirit he casts out devils; in the same power of the Spirit he preaches. He is seen as the instrument through whom there would be an outpouring of the Spirit on all men. 'God had anointed Jesus with the Holy Ghost and with power' (Acts 10:38).

There is no need to explore this matter in greater detail. The point we are making is, that the way in which a Jew of the time would have answered the question as to who Jesus was, would have been to relate his life to the Spirit of God. We are told nothing as to how this relation is to be conceived, but it was a relation which befitted the uniqueness of Jesus. John Baptist is spoken of as one who was 'filled with the Holy Ghost, even from his mother's womb', but Jesus is superior to John, and presumably, therefore, the relation between Jesus and the Spirit of God must have been thought of as closer even than that. But no explanation is given us of it; but explanation there must be, if any Spirit Christology is to be credible.

One might have expected that serious attempts would have been made to produce a Spirit Christology, and indeed some such attempts were made, all of which proved to be abortive. One of the most interesting of these attempts was made by Paul of Samosata, whose work was condemned by a Synod of Antioch in A.D. 268. Paul's actual teaching can only be found in the biased writings of his opponents, and one must suppose that the odds were heavily weighted against any attempt to explain the mystery of Christ's person which dared to depart from the Logos doctrine. Apparently he insisted on a historical approach in regard to the problem of Christ's person, and conceived of Jesus as a man who was increasingly indwelt by the Spirit of God until he became the perfect man, and was finally rewarded with adoption.

If this is a correct statement of his teaching, it was obviously a wrong interpretation of the historical facts. Adoption is a legal process which cannot be applied to the case of Christ. In any case, an adopted son is not a son in reality, and to apply this human concept to Christ is not only inadmissible but destructive of the Gospel itself. Paul would have been on safer ground, if he had interpreted the facts by saying that Jesus was not the whole of God but as much of God as could be expressed in a human life, and therefore sufficient for us. To say this is to hold that in some sense Jesus was always divine, but this is precisely what Paul's teaching denies. The Synod was right to condemn him on the ground that his teaching did not express adequately the unity between Christ and God. Whilst asserting that Jesus was truly human, the Synod insisted that Jesus was different from other men, and that the difference was a difference in kind and not merely of degree. But, whether the reasoning of the Synod bears a true relation to the historical facts is a matter for examination, and will concern us in the next chapter. Meantime the interest of Paul's attempt lies in his insistence that Christ shall be conceived as a genuine man, and that whatever more is said about him must conform strictly with his history. Paul's point of view has many sympathizers in modern times.

★ ★ ★

To sum up—what we find in the New Testament is a gradual precision of thought as to the mystery of Christ's person. An element of mystery is suggested by our Lord's own choice of the title 'Son of Man', but we do not know enough about it to be sure of its implications. The Easter event took the matter a stage further when Jesus was worshipped as 'Lord'. No doubt this experience influenced, to some extent, the formulation of the gospel tradition, though there is evidence to suggest that the Lordship which Jesus exercised in his pre-resurrection ministry facilitated the post-resurrection ascription of 'Lord'.

Precision reached its heights when, in the prologue of St John's gospel it is declared that Jesus is the Word of God made flesh. Jewish thought at the turn of the century, influenced no doubt by Greek thinking, had arrived at the concept of the Logos of God, denoting the rational principle of the universe, by whom all things were created and sustained. But the traditional Hebraic way of accounting for extraordinary human powers was the concept of the Spirit of God. It is this concept which is prominent in the Synoptic gospels, though it is not worked out. The question at issue is, would it have yielded a more satisfactory Christology than the Logos doctrine?

CHAPTER THREE

## THE LOGOS CHRISTOLOGY

IT was the experience of the Resurrection which, above all else, threw light on much that had seemed mysterious about Jesus, and which led his followers to worship him as Lord. In Palestinian circles a Spirit Christology had served as a natural explanation, but meantime the Church was in touch with the Gentile world, and the strong need was felt for some category of thought which would explain Jesus to Greek-thinking people. So, by the end of the first century, we find the Fourth Gospel adopting the Logos doctrine in its prologue. Jesus was the Logos of God made flesh. In him was incarnated the rational principle of the universe, by whom the universe was created, and through whom it was inspired and informed. The merit of this answer to the mystery of his person was that it justified the worship which Christians were paying to Jesus. They were not worshipping a man, but the Logos made flesh. It had the further merit of providing a category of thought which was familiar and intelligible to the Gentiles.

It is worth remarking that in the Old Testament the Hebrew concepts of the Word and Spirit could be used interchangeably, and meant much the same thing. The Psalmist could declare 'By the word of the Lord were the heavens made', and the thought here is that of the spoken

## THE LOGOS CHRISTOLOGY

utterance of God which carried with it the necessary power of action. In the creation myth of Genesis it is the Spirit of God who is the agent of creation. If the Psalmist could speak of the heavens as made by the Word, the book of Job could say 'By his Spirit he hath garnished the heavens' (26:13). This use of 'Word' and 'Spirit' is very near to the Greek concept of Logos as the agent of creation and as 'the light which lighteth every man that cometh into the world' (John 1:9). The insights provided by the Hebrew thought of the Spirit yield the same values as the insights provided by the Greek concept of the Logos. But the Church chose to develop its doctrine of the person of Christ on the lines of the Logos doctrine, and the primary motive was the missionary interest inspired by its entry into the Gentile world.

\* \* \*

But the Logos doctrine as a basis for understanding Jesus proved to be very difficult, and a comment on its inherent difficulties is the fact that controversy, sometimes acrimonious, spread over four centuries of time, until the final doctrine was formulated and accepted at the Council of Chalcedon in 451. One of the inherent difficulties, which caused endless debate, was the assumption that certain truths were to be affirmed about the Being of God, which must be taken for granted as a matter of reason. It was assumed, for example, that the Godhead must be impassable, incapable of suffering, seeing that suffering is a mark of finite limitation which cannot belong to the Godhead. But this assumption was in open conflict with the fact that Christ, who was worshipped as Lord, suffered.

Another inherent difficulty, in the earlier stages of the debate, was doubt about the Logos, as to whether he was to be thought of as equal to God, or in some way less than God. Still another difficulty was the assumption that what constitutes a man was something that was known. What ought to have determined these issues is not *a priori* assumptions, but the fact of Christ himself, who was held to be the revelation of God, and the exemplar of what ideal manhood actually is.

An early attempt to account for Jesus on the basis of the Logos doctrine was made by Justin Martyr in the second century. The background of his thought was that of a world of corruption ruled by death. Into this world the enfleshed Logos had entered, and had broken the grip of death, and thereby opened the way for mankind, and indeed for the whole creation, to enter into the realm of incorruptibility. This was good news indeed, which made a powerful appeal.

Justin insisted that Jesus was a man like ourselves, but distinct from all other men by reason of the fact that the Logos was incarnate in him. He was truly like us, but his origin set him apart from us. It was right to worship him, for this man was the Logos of God. But Justin's thinking did not do justice to the manhood of Jesus. He was a full man with body, soul, and spirit, but he was without historical relationship to the rest of mankind, because of his miraculous birth and his involvement with the Logos.

> Justin's Christ is like a specimen on the anatomist's dissecting table. It is open to see that all the parts are there, and the specimen is judged to be a fair representation of the species in

## THE LOGOS CHRISTOLOGY

question (Paul M. van Buren, *The Secular Meaning of the Gospel*, pp. 38–39).

Justin could accept the fact that Christ suffered, because in his thought the Logos was not equated with God.

But other thinkers, notably Origen in the third century, insisted that the Logos must be thought equal to God, and at this point the real difficulties began, because what was at stake was the impassability of God. Obviously it was impossible to make such a distinction between the Logos and God, for if the Logos was not God, there could be no assurance that God had really entered into our human estate. A possible solution, which was suggested, was that Jesus did not die but only seemed to die, which, of course, was a flagrant denial of history. Others suggested that a distinction should be made between the man who suffered and died, and the divine Logos who did not. But this obviously denied the unity of the person and had to be rejected.

In the main, and without attempting to go into detail, the debate wavered between those who were concerned to preserve the unity of the person at the expense of the manhood, and those who chose to preserve it at the expense of the divinity. The problem seemed insoluble and indeed proved to be insoluble, and the end of the story was not a solution but a skilful compromise, for this is what the Chalcedonian formula actually was.

\* \* \*

The findings of this Council were made possible by the technical language available through the current Neo-Platonic philosophy. Christ was said to have two 'natures', one divine, one human. He had the nature which makes a man a man, and also the nature which marks the divine in contrast to the creaturely. Nothing that marks true manhood was missing, and nothing that marks divinity was lacking. Everything has not only a 'nature' but also a 'hypostasis'. This is a difficult word to translate, but it may be said to refer to the actual existence which allows a 'nature' to exist at all. The answer of the Council, therefore, was that the 'hypostasis' of the Logos, having a divine 'nature', took on a human 'nature' also. So the manhood of Christ was considered to be constituted of a human 'nature' and the 'hypostasis' of the Logos. In other words, Jesus was truly a man, but his existence as a man totally depended on the fact that the eternal Logos had called him into being.

The formula of Chalcedon ran thus:

> It should be confessed that our Lord Jesus Christ is one and the same Son, the same perfect in Godhead, the same perfect in manhood, truly God and truly man, the same Christ made known in two natures without confusion, without change, without division, without separation, the difference of the natures having in no wise been taken away, but rather the properties of each preserved, and both concurring into the one 'prosopon' (person) and one 'hypostasis' (substance).

So the communion of 'natures' was held to be inseparable, neither losing its identity, such union being preserved by the irrevocable act of God. The divine did not cease to be divine, nor did the human cease to be human, or become absorbed in the divine. All relevant factors are skilfully included in this formula. Its value, according to William Temple, is that it refuses to explain. He holds that it represents the bankruptcy of Greek Patristic theology, and the failure of all attempts to explain the Incarnation in terms of 'essence', 'substance', 'nature' and the like. It is content to affirm the fact of the Incarnation, which is all that can be expected of a formula. Any explanation, he holds, must be inadequate (*Christus Veritas*, p. 134).

But even as a formula, we must remark that it is the product of a philosophy and of a psychology which are long since outmoded. Yet behind all these long-protracted controversies, ending with the formula of Chalcedon, there was a serious attempt to do justice to the mystery of Christ's person and its tremendous significance. What was at stake was the mystery of God's entry into the world, a mystery which involved not mankind only, but the whole cosmos.

> His mighty Word had gone forth and brought into being one piece of a new order: a man born miraculously to be the bearer of the eternal Logos, from which all things had their being. As Athanasius puts it in an analogy, it was as if a king had come to a city and had taken up residence in one of its houses. Forever after, not just that one house, but the whole city could claim the honour and protection of the royal presence (van Buren, *op. cit.*, p. 87).

Because the Chalcedonian statement is a formula and not an explanation, it cannot be said to do justice to the manhood of Jesus. This formula of two 'natures' united in the one 'hypostasis' of the Logos, means that Jesus did not have a human 'hypostasis'. All other men have their 'nature' and their 'hypostasis', but Jesus had not. He is denied the ground of his human existence, unlike all other men.

> He entered into the place where we are, but he was a visitor, not a member of the family (van Buren, *op. cit.*, p. 45).

The Logos doctrine provides an explanation of the uniqueness of Jesus, but it remains a very questionable explanation. The 'centre' of the personality is the divine Logos made flesh, and in that case, whilst the miracles become intelligible, and the kind of language which the author of the Fourth Gospel puts into the mouth of Jesus consonant with his status, what becomes difficult is the Synoptic portrait of a man who was human enough to feel uncertainty and even to err.

In the Fourth Gospel the Logos doctrine has taken full charge. The central figure is the divine Son of God, so that the impression conveyed is that of the Christmas hymn, 'Veiled in flesh the Godhead see'. Few of us can read the dialogues with the Jews, and the kind of language which is put into the mouth of Jesus, without feeling its embarrassing unnaturalness. It can make Jesus say, 'No man hath ascended into heaven but he that came down from heaven.' 'He that cometh down from above is above all.' 'I and my Father are one.' As we read such language, we ask ourselves, Is this a real human being who thus speaks?

What has happened is that the author of the Fourth Gospel has forsaken history to give us an interpretation of Jesus which is inspired by the Logos doctrine. True, John was concerned to provide an interpretation, and we are not saying that his interpretation is untrue, or claiming that everything in the Synoptic gospels is historical, but only that the whole approach of the Synoptists purports to bear the impress of the historical in a way that the Fourth Gospel does not, because it deals with one who was a genuine man, albeit a unique man.

We are claiming that this is the right approach—the

## THE LOGOS CHRISTOLOGY

approach which begins with the human and goes on to the divine, and not the reverse approach of the Fourth Gospel. It is true that the Fourth Gospel, to which we may add also the Pauline and Petrine Epistles, deal with the Christ of faith. But the tendency, through the influence of the Logos doctrine, which must have been operative some time before the end of the first century, is to draw too sharp a line of distinction between the Christ of faith and the Jesus of history.

Such a distinction can have no basis in reality, for the Christ of faith was the Jesus grounded in history, the Jesus who lived and died, as well as rose again. As one of the New Testament writers insists, this is the same Jesus, 'the same yesterday, and to-day, and for ever' (Heb. 13:8).

What we are saying is that the approach of the Logos doctrine is unhistorical, and inevitably leads to a view of the humanity of Jesus which must fail to convince. However true it may be that a proper understanding of the very technical and difficult language of Chalcedon does not justify this criticism, at any rate it is justified when one looks at the Fourth Gospel, and still more justified when one examines popular piety.

\* \* \*

Further, this whole issue lies at the root of many of the difficulties prominent in present-day New Testament studies, which have brought such perplexity and weakening of faith to many people.

Some of these difficulties arise because of 'reduced' Christologies, which go to the lengths of denying the supernatural, and replacing it by the notion of 'myth'. This eliminates the miracles and the Virgin Birth, and produces a treatment of the Resurrection which is highly unsatisfactory, and deeply unsatisfying. It has found support in the work of some of the Form Critics which, in recent years, has been influenced by philosophical presuppositions of which we should be critically aware. If one accepts the conclusions of some present-day Form Criticism, very little of the historicity of the gospels is left to us, in which case Christianity ceases to be an historical religion, and takes its place with the pancreistic religions of the world, which are avowedly mythical.

This is not to deny that Form Criticism is a proper discipline, which has an understanding to make as to how the tradition behind the written gospels was ultimately formed. What we are saying is that some of its conclusions are necessarily tentative, and, in some cases, open to the charge of alien influence which ought not to be allowed to obtrude.

On the other hand, so 'full' a Christology as that represented by the Logos doctrine is also beset with difficulties. The main indictment of it is that it is out of line with the historical; it finds it easy to accept the supernatural, but is ill at ease with the natural. This point becomes impressive when the Fourth Gospel is compared with Mark, which is usually agreed to be the earliest of the gospels. We have to remember that both books belong to the post-resurrection period, and the influence of the resurrection period is to be seen in both, though in John, seeing that this gospel is essentially a theological interpretation, to a much more marked extent.

Mark's gospel for the most part reflects the tradition

## THE LOGOS CHRISTOLOGY

handed down from father to son as to what was known about Jesus, of what he had said and what he had done. This is not to claim that it is all historical, and that the tradition should not be critically examined and tested, wherever it is possible so to do. What we are claiming is that on the whole it presents us with a convincing portrait of the sort of man Jesus was. It belongs to the category of history rather than interpretation, though, as we have said, the interpretative element, inspired by the resurrection event, is to be discerned. The portrait presented is that of a prophet who is not without honour save in his own country (6:4). He disclaims the title 'good' on the ground that it is applicable to God alone (10:18). But his disciples are puzzled about him. 'What manner of man is this, that even the wind and the sea obey him?' (4:41). 'They were sore amazed and wondered' (6:51). But he marvels that they do not understand him. Peter, however, is commended when he confesses him to be the Messiah (8:29). His Messianic role is exemplified when, at the Last Supper, he inaugurates the New Covenant (14:22-25). But the word 'Messiah' does not reveal the whole mystery. He is the Son of Man who must suffer, and after three days rise again (8:31). This Son of Man is to come again in the glory of the Father with the holy angels (8:38). He will come in the clouds with great glory (13:26).

This title 'Son of Man', as we have seen, was original to Jesus himself. It includes all that belonged to the title 'Messiah', but to it also belongs the thought of vicarious service and suffering. Jesus is THE MAN—the representative of his people, and the emphasis is plainly on the fact that his role was human, that of a man. Whether, in his mind, the title implied that he knew he would rise from the dead and come again in the clouds of glory, we do not know. It may be that here the narrative has been influenced by the current Apocalyptic and by the resurrection event.

The general impression, however, of the central figure of this gospel is of a historical and not a mythical figure. All through it he remains a man, albeit a unique man, who could not be holden of death. Mark's portrait is that of a man plus something more which is very mysterious, but which apparently was thought to be intelligible in terms of the action of the Spirit of God.

When we turn to the Fourth Gospel, a very different figure confronts us, even though there are points of identity with the Marcan figure. There is the same Apocalyptic influence, as in 1:51 where Jesus speaks of the heavens open and the angels ascending and descending upon the Son of Man. As Son of Man Jesus is given the authority to judge (5:27). As Son of Man he gives the bread of life (6:11). The people, as in Mark, think of him as a prophet (6:14). They acknowledge him a good man, but some think that he deceives the people (7:12).

But the language which Jesus uses of himself is of another kind. He is the only begotten Son of the Father (1:18). He manifests 'glory' (2:11). He is knowledgeable about heavenly things (3:18), and does not refute the charge that he makes himself equal with God (5:18). He came down from heaven (6:38). He who has seen him has seen the Father (14:9). He is the Light of the world (8:12). He is not of the world but abideth for ever (8:23, 58). He can speak of 'we' in reference to the Godhead, for the Father is in him, and he is in the Father (17:21). He knows all things that

## THE LOGOS CHRISTOLOGY

should come upon him (18:4), and we should contrast this with the human figures in Gethsemane in Mark's gospel. Significantly John omits this scene in Gethsemane. He tells the Samaritan woman all things that she ever did (4:39).

It would be wearisome to add further quotations, but enough has been said to demonstrate that the central figure in this gospel is not primarily a man but the Logos made flesh. The Synoptic portrait begins with man and then goes on to the how much more. The Johannine portrait begins with the divine Logos and then fits him into the mould of a man.

\* \* \*

Our thesis is that a Spirit Christology, which we would claim to be a 'full' Christology, relieves these tensions. It copes alike with the natural and the supernatural, and in the end it yields the same values as the Logos doctrine.

But before we proceed it will be helpful to consider why William Temple could speak of the bankruptcy of Greek Patristic theology. In a footnote (*op. cit.*, p. 134) he observes that it is not the formula which fails to solve the problem, for the formula does all that one can expect of a formula, but the history of the whole controversy. The Greek concepts of essence, substance, nature, and the like, provided no solution, and the failure remains. It had to be said, for example, of our Lord's humanity that it is impersonal and that Christ was Man and not a man. This invites the question, Is there such a thing as human nature apart from individual persons who share it?

Temple frankly confesses that he cannot speak of Christ's humanity as impersonal.

> If we imagine the divine Word withdrawn from Jesus of Nazareth, as the Gnostics believed to have occurred before the Passion, I think there would be left, not nothing at all, but a man (*op. cit.*, p. 150).

The truth is that we no longer believe in the 'real universals' of the Greeks, of which the Logos concept is an example. Our approach is concrete and personalistic, whilst theirs was abstract. We do not believe that there is such a thing as a universal reason which can exist apart from the individuals in whom it is expressed.

Our modern way of thinking would have much more in common with the Hebrew concept of the Word of God than with the Greek. Their concept was concrete and directly personal. The word of a man was the man himself, and yet in a sense separate from the man himself. So the Word of God was God Himself, and yet in a sense separate from God, though never separate in the abstract sense in which the Greeks conceived it.

Clearly William Temple was right in his judgment that Greek Patristic theology failed to meet the problem of the person of Christ. On such premises it was found to fail, and that is good reason for an approach on lines other than that of the Logos doctrine.

CHAPTER FOUR

## A SPIRIT CHRISTOLOGY

WE begin with the thought of our opening chapter of the whole universe as instinct with the presence of God. Creation is an expression of God's eternal activity. It belongs to His very nature to be Creator, and therefore to be self-revealing and self-giving, uttering Himself in and to His creatures. But the Bible never portrays a merely immanental God such as would lead to Pantheism, where no distinction is drawn between God and Nature. The Spirit who is instinct in all creation is always the infinitely transcendent Spirit, the Holy Spirit, who is to be discerned in the good and the true and the lovely. As Pringle Pattison observed:

> It is the immanence of the transcendent, the presence of the Infinite in our finite lives, that alone explains the essential nature of man—the divine discontent, which is the root of all progress, the strange sense of doubleness in our being, the incessant conflict of the lower and the higher self, so graphically described by St Paul as a law in his members warring against the law of his mind. And the more clearly we identify the call of the higher with our true self the more unfeignedly do we recognize the illumination of the divine Spirit (*op. cit.*, p. 22).

★ ★ ★

If God is instinct in creation, the apex and crown of which is the human soul, and if His nature is self-revealing and self-giving, then we would expect the possibility of personal communion between men and the divine Spirit. Goodness, truth, and beauty are values which have meaning only for persons, and, if the influence of the universal Spirit is always associated with these values, the influence must be personal.

In the Old Testament this influence is recognized and acknowledged in many ways and in varying forms. It is seen in the enhancement of natural powers, as in the case of Othniel, who, in a day of national calamity, judged Israel in the power of the Spirit and prevailed against her enemies (Judges 3:10). Wisdom and discernment are seen as specific gifts of the Spirit, as in the case of Joshua, who 'was full of the spirit of wisdom' (Deut. 34:9). Of Bezaleel, in addition to wisdom and understanding, his cunning craftsmanship is also ascribed to the influence of the Spirit (Exod. 31:3). Prophecy is a characteristic mark of the influence of the Spirit. Micah can say 'I truly am full of power by the spirit of the Lord' (3:8), and Isaiah can proclaim 'The Spirit of the Lord God is upon me' (61:1).

The presence of the Spirit is most clearly manifest in the phenomenon of inspiration, whereby certain men become the organs of divine communication to other men. This phenomenon is sporadic and occasional only. It was recognized as having happened in the case of certain individuals or groups, but it was not part of the general and continuous endowment of all God's people. That this would one day happen was the joyful and fervent hope of the messianic expectation.

## A SPIRIT CHRISTOLOGY

What we see here in the Old Testament is men conscious of heightened powers associated always with work which is good and laudable, and, in connection with men who knew themselves to be in touch with a power not of themselves, which they believed to be the Spirit of the living God. Against this background it was natural, therefore, that when confronted with so unique a human personality as Jesus, His followers should have attempted to explain him in terms of the influence of the Spirit of God. They saw this influence in his birth, in his baptism, and as explicatory of all that he was, and did, and said. They also saw in him the fulfilment of the messianic prophecy, which dreamed of the day when the influence of the Spirit through 'him that should come' would be the experience of all God's people.

★ ★ ★

The operative word in this Old Testament picture is 'influence', and to understand it we can turn to our ordinary experience of life, where one man can exercise influence over another. What is the power which some teachers possess, when they manage to transform a pupil of no unusual abilities into one who develops unsuspected powers of understanding and expression? Under this new teacher 'the penny drops', and now he does things which formerly were seemingly beyond his powers. We may say that the spirit of the teacher enters into the spirit of the pupil raising his natural powers to a new and unsuspected level. Or, what is the power of a good friend to influence for good? Again, it is a blending of spirit with spirit, calling forth the good and inhibiting the bad. Or what is the influence of a great orchestral conductor who can impress on his orchestra his own insights and a corresponding power to express them? He does this by word and gesture, but also by a still more subtle influence which once more, may be described as a mingling of spirits.[1]

In all these cases of 'influence' there is no replacement of natural powers but an enhancement of them, so that hidden potentialities are called into being. In the case of each of them, it should be noticed that there is a common reciprocal element. The pupil must show a willingness to be taught; the befriended must reciprocate friendliness; the orchestra must be open to the guidance of its conductor, and in their case there must be the necessary technique. Indeed, some willingness and capacity to respond is common to all these cases where influence is concerned. It can never be operative without this factor of dedication and self-giving.

The same is true in those cases in the Old Testament where the influence, it is claimed, is that of the divine Spirit. Othniel possessed natural powers of judgment which the divine Spirit could enhance and use to good effect. He was already a soldier who knew a soldier's job when God called him to deliver Israel. Again, the prophets were dedicated men, who by their dedication were open to the influence of the Spirit, and capable of becoming channels of its power and inspiration. And if dedication is a necessary quality for such influence, so also is sensitivity. There can be sensitive people who lack dedication, and there can be dedicated people who lack sensitivity, but it is only when these qualities are combined that there is produced the genuine prophet or the genuine artist. Not all great art expresses

[1] I owe these illustrations to C. W. Emmet's essay, 'The Psychology of Inspiration', in *The Spirit*, edited by B. H. Streeter, pp. 199f.

something of the eternal values of the good, the true, and the lovely, but great *creative* art does, and is in fact the inspiration of the Spirit, for the good, the true and the lovely, proceed from the Spirit, who is the creative Spirit.

In the case of the prophets, the inspiration is conscious of its source; in the case of art, the inspiration may be conscious or unconscious. The main motive may simply be a deliberate disinterestedness, but, in so far as this is associated with the good or the true or the beautiful, its source is the Spirit, even though the artist may be unconscious of it.

Inspiration may come in a sudden moment of illumination or it may come through psychic media such as dreams or visions. But genuine inspiration never happens without the groundwork which makes it possible. Sometimes it involves a long period of study, reflection, and laboured struggle. The moment of inspiration may come like a flash of lightning, but it is not the suddenness which authenticates it as genuine, but the dedicatory factor which has preceded it. But once more, both in the case of religious and artistic inspiration, there is no supersession of natural powers, but a heightening of them, and always it is a case of heavenly treasure in earthen vessels, with the latter easily detected. The limiting marks of the merely human are never absent.

\* \* \*

The Biblical explanation of inspiration, which is based on the conviction that the creation is instinct with the divine Spirit, is that the human spirit is a potential meeting point with the divine Spirit, who constantly seeks to make contact with it. It is an explanation which does justice to the claim of the prophet and the artist that the vision, which comes to them in an inspired moment, is essentially a vision from outside, to be explained neither by something inherent in themselves, nor in other human beings.

If we think of Jesus in these terms, the picture which emerges is that of a man of such dedication that his communion with God can enable him to speak of the will of God with utter confidence. His complete dedication was matched by a corresponding sensitivity, so that everything in his own life, and in the lives of others, is related to the fact of God. But, like the prophets, Jesus did not cease to be a genuine human being. He shared with his fellow-men views about the universe which have long since been outmoded; he does not know the will of God in advance but has to seek and be assured of it; he is ignorant of the authorship of the 110th psalm; he shares in the current belief in demons, and he may have shared the illusion that the world was coming to a catastrophic and speedy end. In any case, this factor of ignorance, it can be argued, is what we should expect of a genuine human being, and it in no way invalidates his claim to be God's revelation to humankind, or rather, such revelation as was possible for a human being to make, and therefore intelligible to us, and sufficient.

So in any effort to explain Jesus we have to take account of his human limitations, which included the possibility of error in regard to some matters. A Spirit Christology, we claim, can accommodate itself to this fact, but would it yield the result of the Church's doctrine of incarnation, of the Logos made flesh? Does it adequately account for his uniqueness?

★ ★ ★

## A SPIRIT CHRISTOLOGY

Nobody would dispute the fact that Jesus was unique. Our examination of the various titles ascribed to him by his followers shows at least that he believed himself to be a man called of God to be His chosen instrument. Other men have made similar claims, and usually their sanity has been doubted. But nobody has ever doubted the sanity of Jesus, or imagined him to be deluded in believing himself as standing in some special and intimate relation with God. This is a fact to be accepted and accounted for, and if anybody doubts his sanity, the onus is on them to substantiate their doubt, and they will find it beyond their powers.

If we consider his recorded sayings, the universal verdict is that here is the voice of a most remarkable and unique man. This is a corresponding fact to be accounted for, and it is not accounted for on the extreme view that nothing can be known of the historical Jesus, and that we must ascribe his sayings to the early Church. In that case, one needs to ask who was the supreme genius who put these words into the mouth of Jesus?

We are entitled, of course, to question whether some of the sayings ascribed to him were authentic, or whether, in some cases, we can detect the influence of the Church, as is obviously the case with some of the narrative which we find in the Fourth Gospel. But as a rule his sayings bear the imprint of his own genius, and some of them may well have been preserved even in the Fourth Gospel.

Nor can it reasonably be doubted that he did many wonderful works, including healings. Others too in his day performed healings, but the claim is also made for him that he resuscitated the dead, and exercised lordship over the forces of Nature. Many find this claim hard to accept, but fundamentally it is a matter of historical attestation, which is not always easy to determine. But this claim has to be considered along with the mystery of his resurrection, apart from which there would have been no Christian religion and no Christian Church. Much will depend on the view which is taken of the resurrection, but any view claiming to be Christian must see it as good news for all men, and, like the Nature miracles, as something unique which belongs to the uniqueness of his person. Indeed, we must say that it is impossible to prejudge what this most unique of all men might have done, or what he might not have done. It is only prejudged when alien preconceived notions are brought to bear on these records.

★ ★ ★

One of the facts which emerges from these records is that his character was morally perfect. We are told that he did no sin, yet that he was tempted in all points like unto us. This need not mean that he was incapable of sin, or that he was devoid of the temptations that assail all other men, for to say this would be to deny that he was a genuine man. A better explanation is to say that he was so completely dedicated to the will of God that no temptation to sin could successfully assail him. This is intelligible in terms of our own experience. When a man is conscious that great issues, depending on him, hang in the balance, he will be fortified against any temptation to let the cause down. In this context he will be 'without sin'.

Probably the most startling claim which Jesus made for himself was the right to forgive sins. If somebody injures me, I can forgive him, but, when wrongdoing concerns other people with whom I am not implicated, I have no right to pronounce forgiveness in respect of them. But this is what Jesus is recorded to have done, and it is a divine prerogative. Some have doubted whether the sayings in which this claim is recorded belong to the Jesus of history. They could have been the creation of the Easter experience. But there is no obvious textual or historical reason why they should be doubted, and the claim behind them is not out of line with the general picture we get of this remarkably unique man.

There are some aspects of his existence on which light is thrown by modern psychological studies. Jesus had the power to look at a man and diagnose his ill. We are told that 'he knew what was in man'. This is a strange phenomenon, rare indeed, which belongs to some people, who seem to have the ability to penetrate into the minds of others and extract their contents.

One thinks of examples of telepathy which are commonplace, and here one can draw on personal experience. In my pastoral work there have been many occasions when I have felt a strange compelling urge to visit a certain house for no reason of which I was conscious, except that I knew I must go. And without exception I discovered I was needed and the people had wished I would call. I can think of a mother who was quite certain that something calamitous had happened to her son in Africa on a certain day and at a certain hour. This was confirmed the next day by a cable telling her of the death of her son in an accident, on the day and at the very hour she had known that something calamitous had happened. Such cases of telepathic communication are too well authenticated to be doubted.

Jesus possessed this power to enter into the minds of others to an extraordinary degree. He could look on a paralysed man and know that his condition was not organic but due to a guilt complex (Mark 2:5ff.). Here was an example of his power to invade even the unconscious mind, for the paralysed man was not aware of the cause of his condition.

We know little of the mysterious realm of the unconscious, but it is worth remarking that Jung, as against Freud, held that the unconscious was racial. W. R. Matthews in *The Problem of Christ in the Twentieth Century* (see pages 44ff.) gives good reasons for thinking that Jung was right in his insight in believing that impulses and motives, which belong to the race, spring up into the conscious minds of individuals. This means that, when Jesus penetrated a man's unconscious mind, he was in touch with the racial subconscious, and, as Matthews points out, this would throw light on the Christian claim that he was the redeemer of all men. We may fail to imagine how any human being could endure the experience of knowing and bearing 'the sins of the world', but, once more, we cannot prejudge what might have been possible for him, the Spirit-filled man.

★ ★ ★

We are arguing that the uniqueness of Jesus can be sufficiently explained by seeing him as the Spirit-filled man. But we must return to the question to which as yet we have given no answer, namely, Does this say what the Church said about him when it gave us the creeds? The Council of Chalcedon insisted that Jesus was 'very man', which was intended to mean that he was a genuine human being. It was recognized that, unless this was unequivocally affirmed

## A SPIRIT CHRISTOLOGY

there could be no Gospel. This genuine man, this unique human being, revealed God. This is a minimal statement which all who call themselves Christians would accept. But in itself it is an insufficient statement.

Both religious experience and reason demanded to know the truth of this man's relation to God, and, as we have seen, in the early days two possible answers suggested themselves. One answer, Hebraic in background, saw him as a man indwelt by the Spirit of God. But the Church chose another answer, and declared that Jesus was the Word of God made flesh. Ultimately this answer reflected Greek rather than Hebrew thinking. It has the merit of providing a clear definition of the relation of Jesus with God, for it begins with the thought of the Word or Logos, and then goes on to consider how the Logos made flesh can be a genuine human being. It asserts that Jesus had two natures, human and divine, but only the one divine hypostasis. We have contended that the weakness of this thinking is that it leaves Jesus with no historical connection with the rest of men. It is open to the charge of seeing Jesus as God masquerading as a man, which would equate Christianity with the metamorphoses of pagan mythology. This is certainly not what the Chalcedonian doctrine intended, but also, without doubt, this is what popular piety tends to make it mean.

The merit of a Spirit Christology, as compared with the Logos Christology, is that it begins at the other end—not with the divine but with the human. It sees Jesus as a genuine man who, at every point and moment of his life, was possessed by the Spirit of God. According to the Synoptic gospels this is how the people of his day thought of him. They linked him with the great prophets, but we have to recognize, as Matthews points out, an important difference between his case and that of the prophets (*supra*, p. 81ff.).

With them inspiration was occasional and sporadic; it was only at certain times that they were conscious of the divine inspiration and could declare 'Thus saith the Lord'. But with Jesus inspiration was continuous, and the prime factor in his everyday life and activity. Further, as Matthews also points out, the experience of inspiration for the prophets did not mean the destruction or diminution of normal human faculties, but rather their enhancement or heightening. It did not, for example, make them infallible sources of information about secular affairs. So it was with Jesus. He was not an infallible source of information about anything which did not directly concern his mission to reveal God. He grew in wisdom, as all of us grow in wisdom.

This is the picture we get of him in the Synoptic gospels, and it should not surprise us, therefore, that he should have been ignorant about modern medicine, or Old Testament critical studies, or that he accepted demon possession as an explanation of disease, or that he may have shared the apocalyptic illusion about the catastrophic and speedy end of this world. All these facts belong to his category as a genuine man, but on the basis of a Logos Christology, where there is only the one divine hypostasis, it is difficult to conceive how Jesus could have been anything but infallible in all his judgments. One can search in vain for anything in the Chalcedonian thinking which in any way faces up to the fact that Jesus could be fallible.

If we concede that Jesus was a real human being, we must say that his human hypostasis, to use the language of Chalcedon, was not replaced by the divine hypostasis, but was in such close contact as to produce a unitary consciousness, a consciousness which was human, but at all points in the very closest contact with the divine. This would be in line with the prophetic experience, where the divine operates in and through the human without in any way diminishing or destroying the human.

This would seem to imply that the difference between Jesus and the prophets is fundamentally a difference of degree rather than of kind. The question we have asked is, Would this yield the values for which the Logos doctrine of the Incarnation stands? The facts are, that there is much common ground between the case of Jesus and the case of the prophets, but there is also much that is not common ground, which makes the case of Jesus unique, and the single instance of itself.

This, at least, amounts to a difference of degree which creates a precedent to be found neither before nor since Jesus, and, if we are to abide by these categories of degree and kind, we could say that the difference of degree in this case, by reason of its complete uniqueness, amounts to a difference in kind. But we must do full justice to the difference in degree. A man so possessed by the Spirit of God might still be capable of error in his human judgments, but he would also possess powers corresponding to his uniqueness. We have used the word 'possessed', and it is a word which can also be used of the prophets. In the case of Jesus, however, we would need to add the adverb 'continuously'. According to the Synoptists the Spirit was operative in his existence before and at his entry into the world.

It is this fact of the Spirit in his life, which, according to these records, explains all that he was, and said, and did. At his baptism he becomes acutely conscious of his relation to the Spirit and of the vocation he is destined to pursue. We must assume that this awareness was progressive as he 'increased in wisdom and in stature with God and with man', and this is what we would expect of one who was genuinely human. In the end this Spirit-possessed man could not 'be holden of death'.

We need a word which will be adequate to do justice to the place of the Spirit in his life. We may speak of him as 'indwelt' or 'possessed' of the Spirit, or as 'inspired' by the Spirit, or as the 'Spirit-filled' man. Or, if we borrow the language of Chalcedon, we may speak of a 'union' between the human and the divine Spirit. But whatever word we use it must not suggest two centres of consciousness. The consciousness of Jesus must be unitary, and his hypostasis human, but we must conceive the indwelling, or possession, or union, as adequate to express and safeguard the truth that, in and through him, God has entered fully into our human estate. That, after all, was the main concern of the fathers of Chalcedon, who believed they were interpreting the truth of Scripture. It is our claim that a Spirit Christology, which was the original Christology, does this more effectively than does the Logos Christology. It has the merit of conforming to the facts of Christ's human existence, and the further merit, we believe, of helping to make Christ intelligible to men of our own day and generation.

★ ★ ★

But does this approach really yield the values of the Church's doctrine of Incarnation? The Logos Christology was inspired by two motives—by the constraint to offer to

## A SPIRIT CHRISTOLOGY

Jesus Christ the worship which belongs to God, and to the need to find some category of thought which would make him intelligible to the world. This doctrine secured both ends, but, we suggest, at the cost of refusing to face up to the fact that Jesus had human limitations, and to seek refuge in the docetism of the hymn which includes the words 'veiled in flesh the Godhead see'.

A Spirit Christology faces up to the historic fact that Jesus had human limitations, because it begins with the human. But if we begin with the human, do we not end with the human, with the final result little different from the adoptionism of Paul of Samosata? On the contary, a Spirit Christology would, we claim, show us God revealed, or, more precisely, as much of God as can be revealed within the limitations of a finite human life.

On its basis, we could say with St Paul 'God was in Christ reconciling the world unto Himself' (2 Cor. 5:19). It would give us what the Logos Christology gives us—the fact that the human life of Jesus is both expression and reflection of the Ground of all Being, not as the supreme anomaly but as the classic instance. It would give this on the presupposition that the creation is instinct with the presence of God, and that at many points and in many places God has entered into, and continues to enter into our human estate. But to do justice to the uniqueness of Jesus we must say, that in him God has entered into our human estate in a way that is final and complete in its sufficiency, so that this particular entry enlightens all that came before it, or can ever come after it. As John Knox has put it, 'The uniqueness of Jesus was the absolute uniqueness of what God did in him' (*The Death of Christ*, p. 123).

All the values of the Logos Christology are here, but without the serious difficulties inherent in it.

* * *

A Spirit Christology would demand a new look at the present doctrine of the Holy Spirit, and of the Godhead itself, and few will doubt the need of this. Pringle Pattison could deplore the tendency to think of the Spirit as a third agency in the Godhead, distinct from the Father and the Son. He wrote:

> The conception of the Spirit is in fact the final and complete account of the one God, who is the Father of spirits, their Creator, Inspirer, and Redeemer (*The Spirit*, p. 11).

The Spirit is not a 'person' existing independently of God, but a way of speaking about God's reality in relation to all that exists and happens. God as the Spirit is God immanent in creation. But the immanent Spirit is also the transcendent Spirit, whom Christ taught us to call Father. In and through Christ the Spirit, who is God, had acted in a new way.

> What was involved was not an enlargement of God, but an enlargement of man; not the taking of two other 'persons' into the divine society, but the revelation of God's different ways of being God (Alan Richardson, *An Introduction to the Theology of the New Testament*, p. 122).

From Jesus we learn of three ways in which God is eternally God. He is the transcendent Father; He is the immanent Spirit; and He is the self-revealing, self-giving love such as is represented by the term 'Son'.

All these three ways in which God is eternally God are to be seen in him who is 'the portrait of the invisible God'.

## A SPIRIT CHRISTOLOGY

Jesus is possessed by the Spirit, who is the immanent God; his mission is to execute the Father's will, and his own relation to the Father is that of Son.

But how are we to conceive of the relation of Jesus Christ to the Godhead, or, more precisely, what is the relation of the humanity of Jesus to the divinity? This is a problem which defeats any Christology, but it is particularly difficult for the Logos Christology, which conceives of the enfleshed Logos as one who can never be divested of either of his natures. Logically this would demand that Jesus Christ should be placed 'within' the Godhead; but this is difficult, for it assumes that something can be added to the perfection of the Godhead. Actually, though illogically, and in deference to Scripture, the Logos Christology has to see Jesus Christ 'alongside' the Godhead, 'seated at the right hand of the Father'. And the illogicality inevitably threatens the unity of the Godhead. On the other hand, a Spirit Christology would see no difficulty in placing Jesus Christ 'alongside' the Godhead, for that is where the man Jesus properly belongs. But because he is the unique man whose human hypostasis is for ever united with the Spirit, he belongs to the Godhead, and is therefore to be worshipped.

Is this binitarianism? It would only be so, if Jesus Christ was conceived as 'essentially' divine, using this word in the Chalcedonian sense. It would not be so if, as a Spirit Christology would suggest, Jesus Christ is to be worshipped, not as a man (which would be idolatry) but as the Spirit-filled man, as the man whose human spirit is for ever united with the divine Spirit. In his earthly existence the Spirit was no more separated from the Godhead, than the Spirit was separated from the Godhead in His relations with the prophets. Jesus Christ as the Spirit-possessed man represents one of the ways in which God is eternally God.

It is fundamental that a true doctrine of God should secure the unity of the Godhead, and we are suggesting that the language of 'persons', however refined and defined, tends, particularly in the sphere of worship, to imperil that unity.

This is a fact which has been increasingly appreciated. It is understood that the Greeks did not mean by their term 'person' what we mean by a person. We mean by a person an individual self-consciousness, but neither the Greek *hypostasis* nor the Latin *persona* meant this. In an attempt to say just what the Greeks did mean, Liddon suggested that all we are justified in saying about the meaning of their language is that the three 'persons' represent 'three eternal distinctions, anterior to and independent of any relation to created life' (*The Divinity of our Lord*, p. 33). We may compare this with A. R. Vidler, quoting C. E. Raven:

> It would be nearer the truth to say that the doctrine of the Trinity means one God, existent in and manifested under three eternal modes or aspects of being (*Christian Belief*, p. 68).

This is helpful, but it does not cope with the problem of Jesus Christ 'seated at the right hand of God', and there is no solution of this problem on the basis of a Logos Christology. We must be able to say that we worship one God, and that we worship Christ as the 'portrait' of the one God. But in saying this we do not worship two Gods, and we would reject any notion that a Spirit Christology results in binitarianism.

But is the resultant doctrine unitarianism? If by unitarianism is meant a doctrine of God which conceives of

Him as a monad, so self-sufficient that He is entirely independent of His creation, then the answer is emphatically in the negative. We have argued, as did Christ himself, that it belongs to the very nature of God to be Creator, i.e. to be the self-revealing, the self-giving, and the self-sacrificing God. This is a truth which the 'portrait' teaches us. It means that creation is an eternal act, and, if the ultimate definition of God is love, then the divine life is essentially a process of self-communication, a life in and through others.

In any attempt to speak of the mystery of the Godhead we are very much at the mercy of our finite language, but enough has been said to support the claim that a Spirit Christology could yield a more satisfactory account of the mystery of Christ's person than is the case with the Logos doctrine. We are also suggesting that it could open the way to a more intelligible, and therefore a more satisfactory and satisfying doctrine of God than is the case with our present doctrine of the Trinity as formulated on the basis of the Logos doctrine. All will agree that it is fundamental to preserve the unity of the Godhead in a way which can be expressed in worship, and which could be free of the metaphysical subtleties of an outmoded philosophy.

We are not presuming to offer a metaphysic of the Godhead in terms of a Spirit Christology. This will require the co-operation of many minds. As Dr Matthews has observed:

> The interpretation of fresh insights and the translation of the truth from one idiom to another will be a long and painful process; but it is a necessary and urgent work upon which we ought to enter not with dread but with eager confidence (*op. cit.*, p. 64).

CHAPTER FIVE

## THE RESURRECTION

It was the Easter event, and the personal experiences belonging to it, which convinced the followers of Jesus that God Himself was deeply involved in the person of Jesus, both in his words and in his work. It was this experience, above all others, which led the Church to offer him worship, and finally to express his meaning by describing him as the Word made flesh. So the Resurrection was decisive for Christology, but our thesis has been to ask the question, Is this Logos doctrine the right Christology?

Its merit is that it is a 'full' Christology, which does justice to the fundamental Christian belief that God has really entered into our human estate in a manner which is final, and, as complete as to meet all our human needs. Christ, we must say, was as much of God as can be expressed in a finite human life, and is therefore sufficient. 'Reduced' Christologies, which get no further than seeing Christ as 'the man for others', fail to do justice to this divine side, and are compelled to reduce the Easter event to a mere change of outlook on the part of the disciples, or as Professor Lampe observes,

> in the manner of a Bultmann to a decision on our part, at this present time, to accept as our Lord the Christ who encounters us in the Easter preaching of the Church, whilst the whole

question of an event alleged to have happened two thousand years ago is irrelevant (*The Resurrection*, G. W. H. Lampe and D. M. MacKinnon, pp. 30-31).

But the difference between a Logos and a Spirit Christology is not the difference between a 'full' and a 'reduced' Christology. A Spirit Christology is a full Christology, yielding all the values of the Logos doctrine, but, as we have claimed, bearing a better historical relationship to the relevant facts. Our criticism of the Logos Christology is that its doctrine of the manhood of Christ is deficient. With the Logos as the 'centre' of the person, it becomes difficult to associate the infallible Logos with anything that suggests human weakness, and the difficulty is greatly increased when we consider seriously the fact that Jesus died.

Remembering that the human hypostasis is replaced by the Logos, how could Jesus, the whole man, die? The Fourth Gospel records Jesus as saying 'I have power to lay down my life and to take it up again' (10:18). But not even God can do the impossible; not even God 'can lay down his life'. This was a problem which greatly bothered the Fathers. They stoutly resisted all docetic notions of the death, and held firmly to the fact that Jesus really did die. But they never solved the problem, and indeed it is inherently insoluble on the basis of the Logos doctrine.

But this difficulty does not belong to a Spirit Christology, which begins with the human and goes on to see the divine in and through the human. It has no difficulty in accepting the fact that Jesus really did die, and whilst, like the Logos doctrine, it can offer no explanation of the fact that 'he rose again', it can, I think, suggest an approach which is credible. It is with this thought in mind that we attempt a review of the evidence for the Easter event which, we believe, may strike a note of vitality.

* * *

In 1966 the then Dean of St Paul's, Dr W. R. Matthews, reissued a little book which he had published as far back as 1936, entitled *The Hope of Immortality*. He ends this book which, to some extent he has rewritten, by a prayer that 'it may help some to become aware of their own mysterious personalities, to know and feel that they are immortal, and to apprehend the revelation of eternal life in Christ' (p. 66). Commenting on the impressive fact that belief in an afterlife is wellnigh universal, he states his view that the most probable explanation is 'that man has always had a dim perception of his own nature, an intuition of the imperishable character of his soul or mind' (p. 20). He points out:

> You cannot conceive yourself as not existing. You can quite easily conceive that other persons do not exist: you have only to think of the world as going on without them. Perhaps you will say, 'Equally well, I can think of the world as going on without me.' Yes; but what you are thinking of then is yourself looking at the world and finding yourself absent. Herbert Spencer used to say that what is inconceivable cannot be true, and I think that, if we accepted that principle, we should have to say that our own non-existence cannot be true (p. 24).

Matthews does not develop the argument in this small book, but he has done so elsewhere.

> The attempt to deal with selfhood as a mere flux or stream of events, or of impressions and ideas, breaks down because the self as experienced is obviously something more than that. We feel and know that we are unique centres of consciousness and activity. We 'have' the ideas and impressions. But when

## THE RESURRECTION

we consider the status in reality of this 'centre', we find ourselves in difficulties. It does not appear to be part of the events which are presented in its experience, and, at the same time, we cannot conceive it as having any existence apart from the experience. Man is 'the great amphibian'—on one side a native of the world where change rules everywhere, but on the other side mysteriously beyond it. It is remarkable that all the great constructive thinkers, in their different manners, have held that there is a supra-temporal basis for the human self (*The Problem of Christ in the Twentieth Century*, p. 74).

We may contrast this with another point of view expressed by Professor Lampe (*op. cit.*, p. 10), who writes, 'As far as human nature is concerned, when you're dead you're dead, and so was Jesus.' Amplifying this, he adds:

> I believe that when we come face to face with the prospect of death there is nothing in ourselves and nothing built into ourselves which we can trust in. When we come face to face with death I don't think we can say to ourselves as it were: 'Well, all right. This body is going to dissolve, but I am confident that somewhere in me there is a sort of built in "me", a soul, or what have you, which is inherently immortal' (p. 24).

Here are two eminent thinkers who differ diametrically on a matter of fundamental import. Which view is right? It is worth while remarking, that the view of Matthews bears a much closer relation to the view held in the time of our Lord than does the view of Lampe.

No Hebrew would have supposed that the death of Jesus was the end of him for he did believe that there was something built into his personality which was extra-temporal. The spirit which came from God would survive in Sheol. But no Hebrew felt any joy in this prospect. Death to him was 'the great enemy' which disrupted the person, robbing him of the body. The spirit which survived was a mere shadow or shade of the real man, the reduction of the man to an existence to which none looked forward.

The Pharisees sought relief from this intolerable situation by a doctrine of resurrection which was conceived in grossly physical form, and which was rejected by the Sadducees. But not even the Sadducees believed that death was the end of a man. Even they could say that the spirit came from God, and would return to him. To this extent everybody believed that there is something built into the person, which is beyond the reach of physical death. Now apart from St Paul, none of the disciples of Jesus were Pharisees, nor were any Sadducees.

As a Pharisee, we may suppose that St Paul shared the apocalyptic views of resurrection which were held by his party, but, intelligent man that he was, it is difficult to believe that he would not have viewed them critically, and in any case, I find good grounds for believing that his views, as expressed in his writings, were shaped, not by the current apocalyptic, but by the Easter event solely.

The belief of the Pharisees was that one day, at the end of the ages, the dead would be raised in their physical bodies to share the bliss of a heaven upon earth. But, even for them, this was a hope which belonged to the far future, and, Pharisee and non-Pharisee alike shared the universal gloom.

It was against this background that the Easter event happened to shatter completely this universal gloom. The followers of Jesus claimed that the Resurrection of Jesus was a signal victory over death; death proved to have no dominion over him. What was this victory over which they rejoiced with an exceeding great joy? The victory consisted in the fact that Jesus, far from being a mere shade, was alive in the fullness of his person.

He was the same Jesus, wondrously transfigured, but the same, and, when they said he was the same Jesus, they meant that the disruptive power of death had been countered in his case, and that death had not been allowed to claim his body. Because he was the embodied Jesus, he was the same Jesus. Whatever Easter means to us, it can only be appreciated against this its Hebrew background, which, in the words of Wheeler Robinson insisted that 'the body is the man'.

True, it finds no support in the Greek view that the spirit, or soul, is the man. For that view the body is dispensable, and without regret, and is to be regarded as a mere envelope which is happily shed at death. It is an encumbrance, and death is seen as a release from its shackles.

But, as William Temple insisted, Christianity, following its parent Judaism, is a materialistic religion. It does not believe that the warm values for which the body stands mean nothing for eternity. As St Paul observed, 'the body is for the Lord' (1 Cor. 6:13). There is a deep contrast between this warm and human view of eternal life, and the cold bloodless view of the Greeks. And, in this matter of the importance of the body as something vital to what we understand by a man, there is every support from modern psychological study, which rejects any notion that spirit can arbitrarily be separated from body.

The triumph of Christ, then, lay in the fact that the risen Christ remained embodied, and there can be no satisfactory understanding of this unless justice is done to the word which is used in connection with Christ. The Jesus who had died, and was buried, was 'raised' by the power of God. It is never suggested in the records that Jesus raised himself, but always that he was raised by God.

This statement cannot be described as a historical event in the same sense as the crucifixion was a historical event. That Jesus died and was buried are historical events which nobody disputes. But the statement 'he rose on the third day' is an event of another kind. Nobody saw it happen, and we have to say, therefore, that because it was not a historical event in the sense that it was actually seen by somebody, it is an event which is accessible to faith alone.

This does not mean, of course, that something very remarkable did not happen, but only that what did happen was a unique event, which broke into history and at the same time transcended history. The documents which record what is alleged to have happened reflect the belief of the Church in the light of it. Thus, they are not historical documents in the sense that they demonstrate that the Resurrection happened; no documents could ever do that, so we must describe them as theological interpretations of the something that happened. The task of the historian is to see whether this interpretation yields a historical picture which is veridical.

He would need to take account of the fact that, within the circle of the followers of Jesus, there was a remarkable change of mood in the course of a very short period of time. After the death they were bewildered men, and frightened too. Nobody was thinking of a resurrection, all of them believing that the cause of Jesus was lost. After the Resurrection the picture is very different. They are then bold and confident men, reunited and back in Jerusalem, prepared to

## THE RESURRECTION

die, if need be, in witness to the truth, which was that Jesus was alive and that God had raised him from the dead. Nobody can verify that Jesus was raised from the dead, but only that his followers maintained this to be the case, and claimed that he had appeared to them, singly and in groups, on many occasions. In addition to the gospel stories describing these appearances, a list is also provided by St Paul in 1 Corinthians 15:1-8.

It is agreed that this narrative is very early material, which he got from the leaders of the Church in Jerusalem. This would date it within ten years of the Resurrection, and the Apostle, speaking of the more than 500 brethren who were witnesses, observes that the greater part were still alive to testify to the fact. From the point of view of a historian this is evidence of first rate importance.

There is no mention of the empty tomb in this tradition of St Paul's, and this omission is sometimes used as an argument to suggest that the story is an invention of a late date, which should be regarded as mythical. But the argument from silence in this case must be suspected. So radical a critic as Professor Kirsopp Lake asked:

> Was there any reason why St Paul should have supplied these details had he known them? Surely not. He was not trying to convince the Corinthians that the Lord was risen: he was reminding them that he had already convinced them. (*The Historical Evidence for the Resurrection of Jesus Christ*, p. 194.)

And again,

> It is almost as certain as anything which is not definitely stated can be, that St Paul's doctrine of the translation of flesh and blood into spirit implied a belief in an empty tomb (p. 192).

It is very unlikely, therefore, when we think of the source from which St Paul received his tradition, that his account should be contrasted with the stories of the empty tomb in the gospels. It is more reasonable to believe that the empty tomb was included in the tradition he received, and that he did not mention it because it was a fact which his readers took for granted. But, there is more to be said about St Paul and the empty tomb which we shall consider later.

As for the gospels, all of which narrate the fact that the tomb was found empty, we have to remember that, so far as their actual writing is concerned, there is a considerable gap of time between them and St Paul's First Epistle to the Corinthians.

A historian investigating the documents would remind himself that the gospel narratives also represent the tradition which, for many years, had circulated orally until it was written down. He would expect the tradition to preserve genuine historical fact, but also material which may be described as embellishment, some of which might possibly be apocryphal, and some of it myth. We could agree that the stories of angels at the mouth of the tomb in some of the sources is an example of myth, which means no more than that this was a way of indicating something mysterious or supernatural which was involved in this situation.

A historian would also observe that the tradition conflicts at various points and reveals many discrepancies. This may be understandable, for witnesses notoriously do often offer conflicting evidence, and, when the event concerned is a mysterious matter, as was the empty tomb, the evidence is likely to conflict all the more. He would take the view that

## THE RESURRECTION

at any rate these various traditions, or strands of the tradition, are independent one of the other, and that would be a point in favour of treating them seriously.

The various stories centre around two foci—that the tomb was found empty, and that Christ appeared to his friends on many occasions; and, no doubt, our historian would ask himself whether there is any connection between these two foci. We shall argue that there is, but meantime one may wonder what our historian might make of some of the stories of Christ appearing to his friends.

There is a story related by St Luke (Chap. 24) in which Jesus eats 'a piece of a broiled fish and of an honeycomb', and a story preserved by St John (Chap. 21) where Jesus eats bread and fish. Are these examples of myth, and, if so, what would the myth signify? Presumably their purpose could be to combat any mere spiritualistic interpretation of what happened, in view of the fact that the disciples were insisting that the risen Jesus was the same Jesus. No unbiased historian could be sure that here was myth, for he could take the view that in these instances Jesus may have accommodated himself to the needs of his disciples in convincing them that he was the same Jesus.

Similarly, no unbiased historian could judge that the empty tomb was an example of myth, unless he allowed himself to bring pre-conceived notions to bear on his judgment, in which case he would surrender all claim to be an unbiased historian. He would need to keep an open mind about the alleged emptiness of the tomb, and recognize the force of the argument that, if the empty tomb were not a fact, the followers of Jesus could hardly have got away with it. The authorities were interested and concerned about the tomb of Jesus, and the tale that it had been found empty could hardly have survived their critical watch.

He would also reflect upon the fact that the disciples were not at all disposed towards belief in what happened, and therefore they could not have developed their faith from the religious concepts of their environment. It is impossible to make psychological sense of any theory which accounts for the empty tomb as the unconscious realization of a deep-seated wish.

We may sum up the judgment of a historian in this way. These traditions are late and contain many discrepancies. There are obvious signs of embellishment, as, for example, in the tales of angels at the tomb. But the various traditions are independent, and there is no *a priori* reason to doubt that the stories are historical, unless one can be certain they are examples of myth. A historian would keep his mind open about this matter. What is certain about the tradition, viewed as a whole, is that the followers of Jesus were quite sure that he had appeared to them on many occasions, and that they affirmed that his tomb had been found empty.

The appearances, apart from just what their nature might have been, are not in doubt. But the story of the empty tomb *is* in doubt.

Professor Lampe sees a historical reason, outside the gospel tradition, which confirms him in the belief that the story of the empty tomb is a myth. He finds it inconceivable that, had Paul known about the empty tomb, he would not have included it in 1 Corinthians 15:1-8 as a telling piece of objective evidence (*op. cit.*, p. 43). He considers that what we have in this story is 'a casting back, in the form of a narrative about Jesus, of the thought and experience of the

Church in later years, and of its controversies with opponents' (*op. cit.*, p. 47). He suggests further that the invention of the story is most likely to have been the product of reflection on the Scriptures, particularly on Psalm 16:10: 'Thou wilt not abandon my soul to Hades, nor let thy loyal servant suffer corruption' (*op. cit.*, p. 58). Finally, he suggests that because the reality of the presence of the risen Lord needs no external confirmation by the empty tomb, to look for confirmation is 'to seek after a sign which shall not be given' (*op. cit.*, p. 103).

It is clear that this issue of the empty tomb cannot be settled on historical grounds alone. But there are other grounds also to be considered. Full consideration, for example, must be given to the language used about Jesus. His followers claimed that there had been a Resurrection. What was raised? The correct answer is that Jesus was raised, and, as we have insisted, by 'Jesus' it was meant that the whole man survived, not only spirit but body too. And that surely was the significance of the empty tomb for the original disciples. The whole man who had died, and been buried, was now raised, and the empty tomb would appear to belong to this sequence.

This is clearly what the gospel tradition suggests, and, assuming its truth for the moment, we have to ask what happened. No one saw what happened; one never sees the hand of God actually at work, only the after-effects. And, if anybody could have seen what happened, he would not have been able to describe it. Conscious of the infirmity of our language, we should have to say that the physical body was transfigured and taken up into the body of glory. What matters is the end-result, which is that Jesus lived in the fullness of his person, and that the values of his physical body were retained and redeemed in the new dimension of life that was now his.

This, of course, was no case of mere resuscitation, such as is alleged to have happened in the case of Lazarus. There is no question, as St Paul puts it, of 'flesh and blood inheriting the Kingdom of Heaven'.

The risen Jesus was the same Jesus, but also a wondrously changed Jesus, whose person was no longer subject to the contingencies of space and time.

Professor MacKinnon observes most pertinently:

> The Gospel writers make clear that on Easter Day events happened which were qualitatively similar to previous events (*op. cit.*, p. 62).

One such previous event was the Transfiguration, which is recorded by all three Synoptists. Mark says that 'Jesus was transfigured before them' and speaks of his shining raiment 'white as snow; so as no fuller on earth can white them' (9:2, 3). Matthew adds 'His face shone as the sun' (17:2), and Luke, speaking of the three who were with him, says 'They saw his glory' (9:32), and this glory, which was seen in Jesus, is linked with Moses and Elias, who appeared in glory. John omits all reference to the Transfiguration, because for him everything about Jesus is a visible and continuous demonstration of glory. What is alleged to have happened is that the person of Jesus, the Spirit-filled man, was transfigured from this earthly estate to the life of glory.

Here is an event which throws light on what could happen in the case of a man who was the Spirit-filled man. Perhaps it throws light also on the empty tomb, as well as on the miracles which Jesus is alleged to have performed. We may not set arbitrary limits on the powers which might have been possible for one who was indwelt by the Spirit.

So, on the basis of our Spirit Christology, we can affirm that the man Jesus died as all men died, which means that he became a corpse, lifeless matter. At this point, we can only make sense of the situation if we concur in the Hebrew psychology that his spirit survived. But, in his case, it was the human spirit in close union with the divine Spirit, and so we have to imagine the effect of this union on the dead body, and see the result in an embodied person who was the same yet wondrously changed.

This, to be sure, is beyond our human imagining, but at least we can claim with Professor MacKinnon that events qualitatively similar to this event preceded it. And, if the Nature miracles are historical, we have there also an example of the Spirit of God exercising absolute control over lifeless matter for His own purposes.[1]

The Transfiguration may not be disposed of by claiming that it is a post-resurrection appearance projected back on to the ministry of Jesus. This type of facile explanation, so called, is only too common, and all too easy. Professor Lampe does not subscribe to this theory, for in his commentary on St Luke's Gospel in the new *Peake*, his caption on the subject of the Transfiguration is—'The meaning of Christ's glorification through death is demonstrated' (*Peake's Commentary on the Bible*, p. 832). Professor C. H. Dodd's judgment on the narrative is that 'This story contrasts with the general type of post-resurrection narrative in almost every particular' (*Studies in the Gospels*, ed. Nineham).

[1] See Note at end of this chapter.

But Professor Lampe remains unconvinced about the empty tomb, and argues that St Paul's use of the word 'firstfruits' rests on the belief that Christ's Resurrection was not different in kind from that to which Christians may look forward. In our case the physical body dissolves; therefore, such must have been the case with Christ. In the sequence 'It is sown an animal body, it is raised a spiritual body', he argues that 'it' is left undefined.

> Paul cannot precisely tell us, but he is evidently groping after the idea that 'we', that is our personalities, will be re-made by God for a different mode of existence from that of flesh-and-blood body, and yet that in some way we shall retain our identity, and be the same personalities as those which now live in the mode of physical beings. This will be so, even though the physical structure is not raised as such (*op. cit.*, p. 45).

He insists that if we take seriously Paul's words that 'flesh and blood cannot inherit the Kingdom of Heaven', the story that the risen Christ could be handled and ate food must be untrue, for in that case flesh and blood did possess the Kingdom of Heaven (*supra*, p. 46). But this ignores the fact that the body which could be touched, and which ate food, was also the body which could pass through stone walls.

We would agree that 'it' does not refer to the flesh and blood of the body, and, we would also point out that, when the Apostle speaks of the 'sowing' of the body, he cannot have meant the burial of the corpse. The 'sowing' is what we make of the whole tenure of our lives on earth.

It may be true that we cannot define 'it', any more than could the Apostle, but we may recollect that Westcott did attempt to define it. He wrote:

> We cannot understand by 'body' simply a particular aggregation of matter, but an aggregation of matter as representing in one form the action of a particular law or formula of assimilation or combination. The specific law of assimilation or combination is that which is really essential and permanent (*The Gospel of the Resurrection*, p. 144).

If this is what the body means, then we can say that Christ is the first-fruits in the sense that the embodied existence we see in him will be ours by virtue of our union with him. This would suggest that St Paul was so aware of the significance of the empty tomb that his whole argument in 1 Corinthians 15 we may suspect is based upon it, and this suspicion is confirmed by the fact that, believing in the Parousia as imminent, he found himself confronted by the problem of those who would be alive when the Lord returned. What would happen to them? The answer he gave was—just what happened in the case of the Lord; their corruptible bodies would be rendered incorruptible, and they would be 'caught up' into the celestial sphere.

If a study is made of the word 'body' in the Pauline writings, we shall find that the Apostle invariably uses the word 'body' in the Hebrew sense to denote the man. The word occurs in seventy-two places in his accredited writings, and in sixty-four of them it is used in this Hebraic sense. But in 1 Corinthians 15 he allows himself to use the word in the Greek sense of the body as a dispensable part of the person. But it is important to appreciate that he does this deliberately to demonstrate his thesis that no existence is real which is not embodied. On the analogy of the case of Christ he seeks to show that the life hereafter will be embodied and will involve resurrection.

Let us say that a person is a soul, or spirit, plus a body which we may designate 'x', these two factors constituting an indivisible unity. The power of death is to rob the person of 'x', though the spirit survives. But what survives is a mere shadow of the man. In the case of Christ, the power of death to disrupt the person was countered by the Spirit of God, so that in his case 'x' was restored, though also in this case the physical element of 'x' involved its transfiguration into the body of glory. What happened in the case of Christ had to be demonstrated, so that he could be exhibited as the first fruits. In other words, his case was unique, as befits the mystery of his person. It exhibited what would be the end-result for all who would be found in him. The exhibition was a once-for-all affair, and therefore there is no question in our case of flesh and blood not corrupting. What matters is that, in and through the victory of Christ, we shall be embodied, and that we have the assurance that all the warm values for which the earthly body stands will be included in the body of glory, as were his. We would contend, then, that the empty tomb, far from being merely incidental to the full meaning of the Resurrection, is vitally essential to it.

\* \* \*

What was the nature of the 'appearances' of the risen Lord to his followers? We may note that this is the word used in the various traditions, including the Pauline, and never the word 'vision'. We get no help from Mark in this matter, for he merely recalls the surprise of the women in finding the tomb empty, and the ending to his gospel is lost. This is a misfortune from the point of view of a historian, as

Mark's narrative would probably have reflected an earlier stage of the preaching tradition than is the case with the other gospels. But the fact that there were several appearances of the Lord is confirmed by Paul's very early list in 1 Corinthians 15. It includes an appearance to Peter and to the Twelve, which are also noticed in the gospel tradition.

The point is that, whatever critical difficulties may belong to the gospel tradition, there can be no disputing the fact that Christ appeared to a number of people, and that this experience was the major part of the Easter event. The word 'appearance' suggests something belonging to the world exterior to the self, and the word 'vision' is excluded by the fact that these appearances could belong to a number of people at the same time.

It is, of course, tempting to want to link up the experience of the disciples with visions described in the Bible, and with mystical experience. E. G. Selwyn in *Essays Catholic and Critical* suggested that the appearances both to the disciples and to Paul belong to the category of what he called 'exterior visions and locutions' and should thus be linked up with other mystical experiences, which, he observes, are very rare, and always individual.

But these appearances of Christ were not all of them individual, in which case they cannot be linked up with other mystical experiences. Selwyn tried to overcome this difficulty by pointing out that Christ was concerned to commission his Apostolate, which was a once-for-all affair, and that the uniqueness of the visions in his case, in that they concerned a number of people and not merely individuals, was a factor belonging to the uniqueness of Christ. Selwyn's theory is quite unconvincing, but he held it whilst retaining a firm belief in the empty tomb.

It is better to stick to the word 'appearance', which suggests a happening exterior to the self and belonging to the outside world, and not something, as the word 'vision' suggests, which could be projected from inside on to the exterior world. And what we may call the 'concreteness' of the appearances was linked in the minds of the disciples, according to the tradition, with the fact of the empty tomb.

This may well explain why nobody suggested, or even suspected, that there could be any hallucination about the experience. The appearances of Christ were linked with that empty tomb, and it was this which gave rise to the clause in the creed in which the Church confessed its belief in the resurrection of the body, which means the resurrection of the whole man.

St Paul expresses its meaning by his phrase 'a spiritual body'—a strange phrase, which indicates the form of the body in the new dimension of life which follows death. Professor Lampe considers that the appearances of themselves, which he describes as 'the reality of the presence of the risen Lord', need no external confirmation by the empty tomb, and suggests that the kind of insistence we are making is tantamount to 'seeking after a sign which shall not be given'. Professor MacKinnon disagrees, and observes:

> Because I seek after facts I look for a publicly observable state of affairs in the spatial and temporal world, not disclosing, nor containing, but still pointing towards that which is, in my view, necessarily unique and creative (*op. cit.*, p. 112).

These 'appearances' of the Lord were real only to the people who were to carry on his work, and were confined to those in sympathetic rapport with him. Jesus did not choose to appear to a Pilate, or a Herod, or a Caiaphas. Does this mean that these appearances might have been photographic in the case of those to whom they were real? The question, of course, is hypothetical, for there was no photography in those days. But, assuming that a believer could have photographed an appearance of the Lord, what then? The photograph might have been treasured in the circle of believers in much the same way as a wedding photograph would be treasured by the parties concerned. But it could have added nothing to the quality of conviction engendered by the experience itself, and so, in itself, it could have served no purpose from the Lord's point of view. But might it not have possessed an evangelistic power?

The answer is, that, if Christ had willed to appear to unbelievers, he would have done so. He had already expressed his feelings on this matter in one of his parables, where he is recorded as saying, 'If they hear not Moses and the Prophets, neither will they be persuaded though one rose from the dead' (Luke 16:31). We must say, therefore, that this hypothetical question is irrelevant to the situation.

There remains, finally, to consider the case of St Paul, and to examine the experience which came to him. For some time Saul of Tarsus had led the persecution of the Church, and was fanatically engaged on his task when he found himself confronted by the Christ, and so potently that the whole course of his life was thereafter changed. This experience apparently was not shared by his companions bent on the same task as himself. It happened to him because there were deep-seated factors in his own personal situation which were absent in theirs, and which prepared the way for what happened in his own case. He knew, of course, what the Christians were claiming for Christ; indeed, that was why he was persecuting them. But evidently at that moment he was a deeply disturbed person. The disturbance may have been less than conscious, but evidently it was manifested in a feeling that he was 'kicking against the pricks'. The Lord needed this man, and his condition was ripe for the experience which came to him.

Was this experience identical with the 'appearances' to the disciples, or should it more properly be described as a vision to be compared with other visionary experiences which are well attested in the Bible and in history? Paul himself equates his experience with that of the disciples. He said, 'In the end he appeared even to me, though this birth of mine was monstrous, for I had persecuted the Church' (1 Cor. 15:9). He regarded the experience as a call to the Apostolate, and saw his own particular destiny as the Apostle to the Gentiles. The Apostles accepted the validity of his claim and presumably accepted his experience as identical with, or, at least, similar to their own. Writing to the Corinthians, Paul could say, 'Am I not an Apostle? Did I not see the Lord?' (1 Cor. 9:1).

There are three fragmentary traditions of what happened on the Damascus road which are preserved in the 9th, the 22nd and the 26th chapters of the Acts of the Apostles. The traditions differ in detail, but all record that Paul saw an exceedingly bright light, and that he heard a voice which he knew to be that of the Christ. The bright light presumably enveloped the figure of the Christ, because he could claim that he had 'seen' the Lord. As to his companions bent on the same mission of persecution, the traditions conflict. In the 9th chapter it is not said that they saw the light, only that 'they heard the voice, seeing no man', and that they stood speechless. In the 22nd chapter they see the light but hear no voice. In the 26th chapter they see the light and fall with Paul to the ground, but nothing is said as to whether they heard the voice.

The interest of these accounts is that they make it plain that the experience of Paul was not merely an inner experience in which only he himself was concerned. It was like the experience of the disciples, in that there were elements in it which were concrete, belonging to the world external to himself, and, in this case, some of these concrete elements were experienced by his companions, though not in a way which could necessarily result in their conversion. This seems to me to rule out any facile psychological explanation of his experience, including the suggestion that his blindness was psychological, and not a temporary condition caused by the blinding light, as the narrative suggests. In a word, this experience of St Paul's belongs to that unique class of 'appearances' associated with the Easter event, which we see in the case of the disciples. There seems no good reason, therefore, to doubt the claim of the Apostle that the Lord had 'appeared' to him as he had 'appeared' to the disciples. And if Paul's experience cannot be properly described as a 'vision', neither can the experience of the disciples.

Professor Lampe lays much stress on the exemplary side of Christ's work, and to the extent that he would exclude the empty tomb as an experience which we do not share, and further, to the extent of holding that all the appearances, including that to Paul, were visions of a type of which there are many examples in the Bible and in history. Professor MacKinnon defends the element of uniqueness and writes:

> If we suppose something done here once-for-all, we will not be surprised to find in the manner of the Amen spoken to that work an element of the unique (*op. cit.*, p. 84).

He feels that the exemplarist approach 'is in crucial respects too relative and limited to offer a wholly significant guide post to men and women in all the circumstances of their lives' (*supra*, p. 76). In the light of the relevant facts, with this judgment one would agree.

## Note on Miracles and the Resurrection

The argument advanced is that no arbitrary limits are to be set to the powers of the Spirit-filled man, who is unique.

If we are prepared to accept the records as historically trustworthy, and see good reason for being critical of devices which explain the miracles away, then we have to consider that the Spirit-filled man (1) could exercise lordship over Nature. By the power of the Spirit he could so react on lifeless matter as to multiply food, still the elements, and resuscitate a dead body; (2) by the power of the same Spirit he could transfigure his earthly existence into the supra-earthly existence of the patriarchs, who were long since dead.

Neither of these categories does more than throw light on the mystery of the resurrection. Resuscitation is not resurrection, and the Transfiguration concerned a body which was alive.

But together, they suggest that it is not incredible to imagine that the power of the Spirit could effect what is

## THE RESURRECTION

indicated by the word 'resurrection'. The same element of mystery belongs to all these occurrences—the mystery of what might be possible for so unique a man as Jesus. In the case of the Resurrection, this statement would be consonant with the Scriptural insistence that it was God who raised him from the dead, for with a Spirit Christology this means that the Spirit raised him from the dead. But on the basis of the Logos Christology it is difficult to conceive that this Scriptural insistence makes sense, for it is incredible that the God-man could 'be holden of death', seeing that God cannot die. In that case, it could not be said that God raised him from the dead. This seems to me to be an insuperable difficulty for the Logos doctrine.

CHAPTER SIX

# THE GOSPELS AND A SPIRIT CHRISTOLOGY

ANYONE who attempts an exercise in a doctrinal formulation of the person of Christ can only do so on the basis that the relevant material is trustworthy. He must be able to feel that, on the whole, the narratives comprising the Synoptic gospels yield a reliable picture of the Jesus of history. If he cannot feel this, and if he has to speak of 'the Christ myth', which suggests that what the records tell us of Jesus corresponds to no historical reality, then he is left with a Christ of faith about whom he can say nothing.

I confess with W. R. Matthews my utter inability to understand the position of those who hold this point of view. I do not doubt that they are very good Christians, but I do not understand them. If it is really true that what we read in the gospels corresponds to no historical reality, then we worship—if worship we can—one about whom we can know nothing. In that case it is difficult to imagine how the Christian religion could endure.

But perhaps this is overstating the situation. We shall be reminded that what we have in the gospels is the view of the Church of what Jesus said and did, and this is true enough. But what we need to know is how far this view was invented, and how far does it correspond to historical truth. One would expect an agnostic to speak of the Christ myth, but not a Christian. What is certain is that the early Christians who worshipped the Christ of faith were not worshipping a Christ about whom they knew nothing. The gospels indicate what they believed about him, and it is fundamental to the future of the Christian religion to be able to believe that the portrait they give us is, on the whole, a true and reliable picture.

Let me explain what I mean by a true picture. One of the services which Schweitzer performed was to destroy the suppositions of the Liberal Protestants who were selective in what they were prepared to believe. The result was that they produced a variety of pictures of the historical Jesus, all of them different. We must take the records as they are, and recognize that they represent what the earliest Christians believed about Jesus. This does not mean that we are compelled to accept everything in these records as authentic. There is frequently a textual problem; it is possible to detect here and there cases of embellishment in the process of transmission; we have to take account of whatever is assured in critical examination. But, even so, a clear picture emerges of what these earliest Christians believed Jesus to have said and done, together with their conviction as to who he was.

The alternative is to decide whether we can accept the picture they have given us, or to think it so unreliable and theologically biased as to produce historical scepticism. In this latter case, we must confess that little or nothing is certain about the Jesus of history. The point can be made that, if those closest to Jesus did not tell us the truth about him, then nobody can, and the question can be pressed, What motive could have operated in such a way as to produce a picture which cannot be taken seriously?

Our concern here is with the Synoptic gospels, which are to be differentiated from the Fourth Gospel on the ground that the latter, unlike the former, deliberately sets out to be a theological meditation, based on the theme that Jesus was the Messiah, the Son of God, and, for St John, the enfleshed Logos. The Synoptic gospels are very different structures, which purport to give us historical detail, but detail seen in the light of the Easter event. They relate the detail and then adjudge its theological significance. The Fourth Gospel states the theology and then chooses material to justify it. So our proper concern in dealing with a Spirit Christology is not the Fourth Gospel, which is really a meditation on the Logos doctrine, but the Synoptic gospels which appeared before this doctrine had won wide acceptance.

In connection with the Synoptic gospels we have to remind ourselves of certain well known and accepted facts. One such fact is that for a number of years nothing was committed to writing about the historical Jesus. The reason for this, no doubt, was the imminent expectation of the Parousia. Stories of his life and death, of what he had said and done, were handed down from mouth to mouth, and also formed the material for the preaching and teaching office of the Church. This continued until about the year A.D. 65—little more than a generation after the Lord's death—when some of the material was committed to writing in the appearance of St Mark's Gospel. Now a good deal depends on how we suppose these stories of what Jesus had said and done survived the passage of time, and also on what view we take of the early Christian community.

It is surely reasonable to believe that these stories would be valued for themselves, and that every care would be taken to preserve the purity and accuracy of what Jesus had said and done, not only because he was Lord and Saviour but also because he was the greatly beloved friend and brother. We have to remember in this connection that after little more than a generation there must have existed some people at least who had seen and heard Jesus. W. Manson in his *Jesus and Messiah* argued that

> the level of intelligence in the original Christian groups and circles must have been relatively high. It rested upon Jewish standards of education, and the conservative mentality of the *Beth-ha-Midrash* may be considered to offer a closer analogy to that of the Church than the naïve creativeness of a primitive story-telling society (p. 27).

The same point has been more recently made in *Memory and Manuscript*, by the Swedish theologian Birger Gerhardsson, who calls attention to the care which the first Christians took to memorize, and then pass on in a pure form the authentic event.

But that the words and deeds of Jesus were valued in and for themselves, and that great care would be taken to preserve their purity, is not the view of some of the Form Critics. According to R. H. Lightfoot such traditions were valued for their importance in solving problems connected with the life and needs of the young churches. Such traditions were finally written down and took fixed form through constant repetition, and to some extent they can be classified according to their type or form (*History and Interpretation of the Gospel*, pp. 30–31). The net result of such an assumption is a picture which affords us very little assured knowledge of the historical Jesus. And it *is* an assumption because it assumes we know just what sort of a community constituted the early Church. But this is something which we do not know.

Nor is any such assumption substantiated by the various forms which are suggested, for these find no general acceptance. Bishop Stephen Neill makes the point

> The question at once arises whether the classification really arises out of the narrative itself, or whether it has been imposed upon it (*The Interpretation of the New Testament*, p. 246).

But the tradition was not wholly oral, for some of it, especially a collection of sayings of Jesus, appears to have been written down at a very early date, and possibly in the lifetime of Jesus. This written tradition (Q) is incorporated in the first and third gospels almost word for word.

Account has to be taken of other factors in reference to the problem of authenticity. Matthew's gospel incorporates a late source, which, just because it is late, needs to be critically examined. Late material may show signs of embellishment, and we would suspect, for example, that the story of the resurrection of the saints at the death of Jesus which belongs to this source, is an example of embellishment, and that it is either apocryphal, or an example of myth. Luke also has his own special source which is also late and which needs to be critically examined.

Another factor of importance is the influence of the Resurrection experience, as to how far it could have inspired sayings which derive from this experience rather than from the historical Jesus. Jesus made confident predictions about his rising again on the third day, and this could be a reading back into the history of something which belongs to the Resurrection event. To credit Jesus with accurate foreknowledge of the future is difficult to reconcile with the fact that he was a genuine man. We have to be aware of such possibilities as we have mentioned, and one of the services which the Form Critics have rendered is to enable us to be aware of them.

We have no interest in denigrating Form Criticism; on the contrary we acknowledge its importance and helpfulness when it is positive and not merely negative in its approaches. Indeed, there is some truth in the supposition that some of the sayings of Jesus may have suffered as to their original meaning through the factor of controversy in the local churches. The saying about divorce may well be a case in point. It remains a matter of debate because its significance is doubtful, but one may guess that in the original form of the saying Jesus was concerned to hold up the ideal of marriage as a state which should not be dissolved, as the will of God. But by the time the original saying had filtered through the minds of communities which had to deal with problems of divorce, the saying had become a legal enactment prohibiting all divorce. In many such ways Form Criticism, in its positive contributions, has much that is helpful to say. But there are certain negative aspects of Form Criticism, particularly in its continental shape, of which we should be suspicious.

This is particularly the case with the de-mythologizing demanded by Rudolph Bultmann. His philosophical interests cause him to classify all instances of the supernatural as examples of 'myth', in which case every alleged instance of the supernatural is denuded of historicity, including, apparently, the Resurrection itself. It is this type of negative Form Criticism which has produced a historical scepticism which could be destructive of the Christian religion.

It seems clear that we should recognize that 'myth' undoubtedly finds a place in the gospels. The cosmology of the first century is mythological rather than scientific, but this need worry no one unless it be taken with absurd literalism. But this word 'myth' is given a wide connotation, and frequently made to subserve philosophical interests which ought not to be allowed to obtrude, and often the word is used without the precision of careful definition, causing confusion. What is needed is a definition which, whilst defining what is meant by 'myth' in the Biblical material, excludes preconceived influence. We could say that myth is picture language inspired by belief that God is concerned in some particular situation, which says something that is spiritually true, and which may, or may not have some basis in history.

Thus, the assertion that angels are concerned in this or that event is a mythological statement. It is a way of saying that God is concerned, but it hesitates to say this in a direct way because of an overstress on transcendence. Some of the Gospel stories connected with the birth of our Lord are examples of meaningful myth, and such stories are not difficult to detect, and if anyone wants to demythologize them there is no loss to spiritual truth. But when it is asserted that the presence of the supernatural indicates the mythopoeic faculty, we must protest and suspect the influence of preconceived notions.

In line with this mythopoeic treatment of the records is

another of which we should be suspicious. The Hebrew early Christians believed that Christ was the fulfilment of all that belonged to the Old Covenant, and, in this or that event connected with the life of Jesus they liked to see prototypes in the Old Testament Scriptures. This is natural and understandable, but it is quite another thing, and an illegitimate thing, to suppose that events in the life of Jesus were invented by and through the influence of Old Testament prototypes.

I would conclude this brief, perhaps over-brief summary, by saying that there is no good reason for subscribing to tentative and doubtful views which produce historical criticism such as cast serious doubt on the authenticity of the gospels. It may be observed that theological scholarship in this country, whilst recognizing that Form Criticism has a useful understanding to make towards our understanding of the gospels, has declined to subscribe to extreme views which emanate from the continent, and I believe that this British point of view is well-founded.

In other words, I would hold that it is perfectly possible to deduce from the material enough of the truth of the Jesus of history to warrant a doctrinal formulation of the person of Christ. The Biblical material is important, because in and by it we are challenged by the Word of God. But the Word of God comes to us through records which tell us what the earliest Christians believed about Jesus, and unless we can be reasonably sure of their authenticity, there can be no Word of God. Because these documents are interpretation as well as historical fact they include all that the New Testament means by faith, and it is in this realm of faith that salvation lies. But, once more, faith must have its content of fact, and it is the importance of this which underlines the claim of Christianity to be a historical religion.

* * *

It remains to illustrate the bearing of this point of view on some of the important issues which confront us in the gospels, and particularly in the light of a Spirit Christology.

(1) The story of the Transfiguration is well attested, being recorded by all three Synoptic writers. Is this an example of myth, i.e. is it a piece of symbolic writing to affirm the Messiahship of Jesus? Or, might it be a Resurrection story which has been read back into the history? Neither of these two suppositions can claim to be more than guesses. The story belongs to the uniqueness of Jesus, and it is most naturally interpreted as representing what the change from this life to the life beyond death might be in the case of one whose physical body was completely interpenetrated by the Spirit of God. Far from being a case of a Resurrection story read back into the history, it is more reasonably viewed as an event in the life of the Spirit-filled man which throws light on his Resurrection. There is no sound reason for doubting its historicity.

(2) Is the story of the Ascension an example of myth? If it is assumed that the Resurrection and the Ascension are not separate events, but that the Ascension is no more than a case of Christ parting or disappearing from his followers, then Luke's account in the Acts could be regarded as an example of myth. But there is a textual problem here which needs to be considered. In his gospel, Luke is content to describe what happened on the day of the Resurrection, and he ends his account by relating that Jesus blessed his disciples, 'and

was parted from them'. This may indicate no more than that this was one of the many occasions when Christ suddenly disappeared, for the words 'and was carried up to heaven', omitted correctly by the *NEB*, are absent from the best manuscripts, and are undoubtedly a late addition.

In the Acts of the Apostles, Luke records a tradition that the appearances of Jesus continued over a period of forty days, and ended with a final appearance, which indicated that the earthly phase of the ministry was finished and was now to give place to a heavenly ministry, where he would be 'seated at the right hand of God'. Not only is this Jesus one who could not be holden of death; he is also one who would reign in the heavenly places. This truth was cogently suggested by what Jesus is alleged to have done. In accommodation to the outlook of his followers he was lifted up and was hidden to sight by the divine Shekinah.

There is no need to make heavy weather about the outmoded cosmology. Christ was concerned to indicate a fact of vital import, and his accommodation to popular outlook was an effective way of doing so. Talk of a physical body making a space-trip to heaven is as irrelevant as it is a case of pretty bad taste. Nobody supposes that the risen body of Christ was a physical body of flesh and blood, and the symbolism of going up has nothing to do with any notion of heaven as a place 'up there'. If Luke's account of the forty days ending with the Ascension is accepted as a true tradition, and it was so accepted by the Church, the supposition of myth is ruled out.

(3) Are the miracles, or any of them, mythical statements? These stories have been preserved by the Church as belonging to the picture which enabled them to know the Christ

of faith, and although the tradition of these miracle stories could have been influenced by the Resurrection event, there is no sound reason for thinking that these alleged events did not happen. Without controversy, the earliest Church believed them to have happened. But each narrative has to be critically examined, and in the case of one at least—the cursing of the fig tree—it looks as though what was originally a parable has, in the process of transmission, become a miracle. The present form of the story could therefore be regarded as mythical.

Stories of healings which Christ performed cause no difficulty, partly because similar healings were performed by others in his day, and partly because by modern psychological standards they can be seen as events which can belong to human skill.

The Nature miracles stand in a different class. Jesus is reported to have resuscitated a dead body, to have stilled a storm, and to have multiplied a small quantity of food to feed a large gathering of people. Attempts to rationalize these Nature miracles are usually artificial and unconvincing, and the point at issue is whether Christ really did exercise lordship over Nature.

Whether we think of him as the enfleshed Logos, or as the Spirit-filled man, he is unique, and we have no means of pre-judging what a unique person such as he might or might not be able to do. There can be no doubting that the Church believed he exercised lordship over Nature, and a good case can be made for believing that the title 'Lord' was ascribed to him before his death.

We may observe that the old rationalistic argument against miracles on the ground that they violate law, is no longer tenable. What is called 'miracle' is the divine initiative within a sphere of law which is already divine law. We can observe how God normally works, and this is what we mean by 'law'; but we have no right to suppose He might not work in other ways, if other ways suited His purpose. What we call 'law' is our observation of sequences which are normally regular and without exception. But such sequences are not something which stand over against the purpose of God; they are expressions of His will, and what we call 'miracle' would also be an expression of His will. The question whether there are occasions when God might choose to act in some way not covered by what we know as natural law is a matter not of credibility, but only of historical attestation.

(4) The nativity narratives, recorded in the first and third gospels, but not by Mark, pose a difficult historical problem. They represent traditions which circulated in the regions from which these gospels had their origin, and they are late traditions. Matthew's gospel is a thoroughly Hebraic document and must have emanated from a Jewish Christian community. Luke was a Gentile, but also a man in close touch with Hebraic lore. There is some evidence that Luke became acquainted with the tradition that Jesus was virgin-born after his gospel was written, and that he added it rather hastily before it began to circulate.[1] Because both sources are late one might expect a mythical element.

A distinction, however, has to be made between the alleged fact that Jesus was virgin-born, which both sources record, and the stories which accompany this alleged fact.

[1] A thorough examination of the textual and critical issues concerned may be found in Vincent Taylor's *Historical Evidence of the Virgin Birth*.

No one could reasonably doubt that the stories of the shepherds seeing the heavens open and hearing angelic song, of the star that stopped over the place where the Christ child lay, and of the angelic visitations, are examples of myth. But they are meaningful myths which say something significant about the Christ child. This child was for the humblest of men, as also for the wise, for Gentile as well as for Jew, and his birth was an event which concerned the very heavens as well as earth. These are significant myths which could not be shed without loss. And there may be some substratum of history behind the stories of the shepherds and the Magi. But it matters nothing to the fullness of faith, if we agree that these stories are examples of genuine myth.

The case is very different, however, with the alleged fact that Jesus was virgin-born. Is this myth also, as some declare? And if it is myth, what could have inspired it? It is not likely to have been inspired by Hebrew thought, where there was no tradition of a Messiah who would be virgin-born. The Jews did not hold virginity in high regard, and Matthew's quotation from Isaiah 7:14, 'Behold a virgin shall conceive and bear a son', must have come from Gentile influence which relied on the Septuagint translation of the Old Testament, where the original Hebrew word is mistranslated 'virgin'. Nor can this alleged notion of a virgin-birth be accounted for by ascribing it to pagan influence. There is nothing remotely like it in pagan literature. Indeed the only known legend, which does in fact resemble it, is to be found in some of the later lives of the Buddha, which were without doubt borrowed from the Christian story.

It is not difficult to hazard what the inspiration of the

Gospel story was. It was almost certainly the influence of the Logos doctrine, which must have been discussed and applied to Jesus long before it made its appearance at the end of the century in the prologue of the Fourth Gospel. This doctrine, as we have seen, was of great value in non-Jewish circles for the missionary purposes of the Church. The story of the virgin-birth of our Lord not only befitted the Logos doctrine; the Logos doctrine really demanded it.

But a Spirit Christology would not demand it; indeed it would be a stumbling-block to a Spirit Christology, just because, like the Logos doctrine, it does less than justice to the real humanity of Jesus. As we have seen, it is Luke especially who explains Christ in terms of the Spirit, but, assuming that he did not regard Christ's virgin-birth as a myth, he cannot have realized its implications for his Christology, and this is understandable, if, as is very likely, he came across the tradition at a late date, and added it hurriedly to his gospel. Thus the import of the story, which we must regard as a myth, is the fact that the life of Jesus was unique from the very beginning, and that the indwelling of the Spirit was 'from the womb'.

(5) The teaching of Jesus, which includes his parables, is centred round the thought of the Kingdom of God and what its incidence demands in all that is included in the word 'morality'. Here we find ourselves confronted by one of the most difficult problems with which the records confront us, namely, the extent to which this teaching is bound up with the current apocalyptic.

The genuine humanity of our Lord involves that he should have been subject to intellectual as well as physical limitations and this problem presents an insuperable difficulty for the

Logos Christology. It is sharpened by the apocalyptic interpretation of the gospels made familiar by Schweitzer, who saw Jesus as dominated by the ideas of the Kingdom which were expressed in the apocalyptic writings. He looked for a catastrophic and speedy ending of the present age and the supernatural inauguration of the Kingdom.

If Schweitzer was right, it follows that not only the religious teaching of Jesus but also his ethical teaching must have been coloured by this apocalyptic outlook, in which case his morality becomes an 'interim ethic'. Using this apocalyptic key, Schweitzer was able to give a more or less coherent account of the life of Jesus, making intelligible things which were formerly obscure.

But the evidence of the gospels is much too complex for this single key to fit, for quite clearly a great deal of his moral teaching looked out into the long future, and equally clearly, Schweitzer was guilty of selecting the evidence, just as Harnack before him, and the liberal Protestants, had been guilty of the same fault.

The notion that Jesus tried to force the hand of God through his death is quite out of character with everything that we know about him. This theory has recently been revived by Dr Hugh Schonfield, a Jew, in his book, *The Passover Plot*. It is not a book which can claim serious attention from scholars, but it illustrates the point just made for it presents us with a picture of Jesus which shocks us and is offensive, just because it is a picture which is completely out of character. In this book Jesus deliberately manipulates events to make the prophecies come true in his own person. He is the perpetrator of a massive plot, which very nearly succeeds, a victim of the crazy apocalyptic which circulated amongst the sectaries. Everything is prearranged and manipulated. There was no spontaneity in the devotion of Mary when she poured the costly spikenard over his feet, no act of mercy in the offering of the vinegar in response to the cry 'I thirst', no act of loving devotion in the request of Joseph of Arimathea for the burial of the body. All these things were part of the plot and each was skilfully prearranged by Jesus. Could anything be further removed from the authentic Jesus than all this?

Yet we cannot doubt that apocalyptic has some place in his teaching, though, unique mind that he was, it is most unlikely that he subscribed to these ideas without modification, and, much more likely, that he used them as a vehicle for the truth he was concerned to proclaim. We have to remember that the followers of Jesus were imbued with these ideas, and that their record of his teaching could well have been influenced by them. Indeed, there is evidence that the apocalyptic element has, in some instances, been emphasized in the later formulation of the tradition, and most scholars would agree that the so-called 'little apocalypse' of Mark 13 and Matthew 24 is no part of the genuine teaching of Jesus. This teaching emphasized that the Kingdom, far from being wholly in the future as the apocalyptists taught, was already present—a factor which suggests that he used this apocalyptic teaching for his own purposes, rather than that he subscribed wholly to it.

At the same time, we must accept the fact that there was a future aspect in his thought of the Kingdom, and that he conceived of it as being brought in by an act of God, rather than by an historical development. This was certainly the expectation of the early Church which waited for 'the day of the Lord', and expected it to come soon. But it finally dawned on the Church that the Kingdom had in fact come with power through the action of God in the death and resurrection of Jesus, and in the Pentecostal outpouring of the Spirit.

True, this was not the sort of spectacular divine intervention of which the apocalyptic writers dreamed, and whether Jesus really subscribed to these ideas, and as to how far his subscription went, are debatable points. At least he shared with them the conviction that the Kingdom of God was 'at hand', and saw himself as the instrument through whom it would be established. Without depriving the cross of its heroic quality, we may note the constraint which drove him to Calvary, and the conviction which filled his mind that his death belonged to the mission with which he had been entrusted by God.

The early Church believed that he would return soon, and this belief persisted until it was realized that in fact he had returned, though not in the way they had expected. Did this belief in his early return derive from Jesus himself? This is something we do not know, but let us suppose that it did, and that Jesus was mistaken. The Logos Christology finds great difficulty here, because it cannot concede that the God-man could have been mistaken. But a Spirit Christology could take the view that as genuine man Jesus might have been mistaken, as to detail, without this limitation seriously affecting his claim to be the revelation of God. It could point out that the creative ideas of the crisis of the present age, and the coming intervention of God to reverse the process, were not mistaken. Crisis there certainly was, for great spiritual issues for all mankind were at stake. And the process *was* reversed by the emergence of the Christian Church.

Crisis, catastrophe, and a divine act of redeeming power—these were the central ideas of Jesus's teaching on the coming Kingdom—and they were all true (W. R. Matthews, *Essays in Construction*, p. 122).

# BOOKS CITED IN THE TEXT

| | Page |
|---|---|
| BUREN, PAUL VAN, *The Secular Meaning of the Gospel*, S.C.M., 1963 | 9, 50–53 |
| DAVIS, CHARLES, *God's Grace in History*, Collins, 1966 | 30 |
| DODD, C. H., *Studies in the Gospels* (ed. Nineham), Blackwell, 1955 | 93 |
| GERHARDSSON, BIRGER, *Memory and Manuscript*, Copenhagen, 1964 | 107 |
| HARNACK, A. VON, *What is Christianity?*, Ernest Benn, 5th edn, 1958 | 18 |
| HEALEY, F. G. (ed.), *Prospect for Theology*, Nisbet, 1966 | 7 |
| JENKINS, DAVID, *Guide to the Debate about God*, Lutterworth Press, 1966 | 26 |
| KNOX, JOHN, *The Death of Christ*, Collins, 1959 | 75 |
| LAKE, KIRSOPP, *Historical Evidence for the Resurrection of Jesus Christ*, Williams and Norgate, 1907 | 87 |
| LAMPE, G. W. H., and MACKINNON, D. M., *The Resurrection*, Mowbray, 1966 | 80–81, 90–95, 98, 102 |
| LEWIS, C. S., *Surprised by Joy*, Bles, 1955 | 28 |
| LIDDON, H., *The Divinity of our Lord*, London, 1867 | 78 |
| LIGHTFOOT, R. H., *History and Interpretation of the Gospel*, Hodder and Stoughton, 1935 | 107 |
| MANSON, W., *Jesus and Messiah*, James Clark, 19 3 | 107 |
| MATTHEWS, W. R., *The Problem of Christ in the Twentieth Century*, Oxford University Press, 1950 | 7, 70–72, 79, 82–83 |
| *The Hope of Immortality*, Epworth Press, 1966 | 82 |
| *Essays in Construction*, Nisbet, 1934 | 121 |

## BOOKS CITED IN THE TEXT

NEILL, STEPHEN, *The Interpretation of the New Testament*, Oxford University Press, 1964 — 108

PRINGLE PATTISON, A. SETH, *The Spirit* (ed. B. H. Streeter), Macmillan, 1922 — 29–30, 61, 76

RICHARDSON, ALAN, *An Introduction to the Theology of the New Testament*, S.C.M. Press, 1958 — 76

SCHONFIELD, HUGH, *The Passover Plot*, Hutchinson, 1965 — 118

SELWYN, E. G., *Essays Catholic and Critical*, S.P.C.K., 1926 — 97

TAYLOR, VINCENT, *Historical Evidence of the Virgin Birth*, Clarendon Press, 1920 — 115

TEMPLE, WILLIAM, *Christus Veritas*, Macmillan, 1924 — 53, 59–60
*Personal Religion and the Life of Fellowship*, Longmans, Green, 1926 — 8, 24

VIDLER, A. R., *Christian Belief*, S.C.M. Press, 1950 — 78

WESTCOTT, B. F., *The Gospel of the Resurrection*, Macmillan, 6th edn, 1888 — 95

# INDEX

Apocalyptic, 24–26, 117–121
Appearances, 96–99; to St Paul, 99–102
Ascension, 112–113

Birth narratives, 115–117
Body, 94–96

Chalcedon, 51–55, 72
Christ-myth, 104–105
Christologies, reduced and full, 55–56, 80–82

Death of God, 32–33

Empty Tomb, 87–88, 90–96

Form Criticism, 56, 107–110

Immanence and Transcendence, 16–30, 61
Impassability, 82–84
Inspiration, 62–66, 71–74

Kingdom of God, 119–121

Lord (Kurios), 37–39

Parousia, 106
Paul of Samosata, 9–10, 45–46

## INDEX

Messiah, 35–36
Miracles, 113–115
Myth, 110

Sacred and Secular, 30–31
Son of God, 36–37
Son of Man, 39–41

Trinity, doctrine of, 76 ff.

Word (logos), 43–44